Quilled Flowers

Quilled Flowers

A GARDEN OF 35 PAPER PROJECTS

Alli Bartkowski

LARK CRAFTS
Asheville

Editor
Beth Sweet

Art Director
Kristi Pfeffer

Photographer
Stewart O'Shields

Cover Designer
Kristi Pfeffer

LARK CRAFTS

An Imprint of Sterling Publishing
387 Park Avenue South
New York, NY 10016

If you have questions or comments about
this book, please visit: larkcrafts.com

Library of Congress Cataloging-in-Publication Data

Bartkowski, Alli.
  Quilled flowers : a garden of 30 paper projects / Alli Bartkowski.
      p. cm.
  Includes index.
  ISBN 978-1-4547-0120-0 (pb-trade pbk. : alk. paper)
  1. Paper quillwork. 2. Paper flowers. I. Title.
  TT870.B2422 2012
  745.592--dc23

                                    2011030852

10 9 8 7 6 5 4 3 2   *2012*

        AUG

Published by Lark Crafts
An Imprint of Sterling Publishing Co., Inc.
387 Park Avenue South, New York, NY 10016

Text © 2012, Alli Bartkowski
Photography © 2012, Lark Crafts, an Imprint of Sterling Publishing Co., Inc.
Illustrations © 2012, Lark Crafts, an Imprint of Sterling Publishing Co., Inc.

Distributed in Canada by Sterling Publishing,
c/o Canadian Manda Group, 165 Dufferin Street
Toronto, Ontario, Canada M6K 3H6

Distributed in the United Kingdom by GMC Distribution Services,
Castle Place, 166 High Street, Lewes, East Sussex, England BN7 1XU

Distributed in Australia by Capricorn Link (Australia) Pty Ltd.,
P.O. Box 704, Windsor, NSW 2756 Australia

If you have questions or comments about this book, please contact:
Lark Crafts
67 Broadway
Asheville, NC 28801
828-253-0467

Manufactured in China

ISBN 13: 978-1-4547-0120-0

For information about custom editions, special sales, premium and corporate
purchases, please contact Sterling Special Sales Department at 800-805-5489 or
specialsales@sterlingpub.com.

For information about desk and examination copies available to college and
university professors, requests must be submitted to academic@larkbooks.com.
Our complete policy can be found at www.larkcrafts.com.

Quilled Flowers PROJECTS FOR A PAPER GARDEN

Introduction

Welcome to my flower garden! Who knew you could create such gorgeous blooms with paper and a few tools? Step into the world of quilling and discover a paper art that has played a role in creative history for hundreds of years. The intricate, detailed nature of this practice produces stunning results from the smallest petal to a breathtaking field of blossoms. But here's a paper gardener's secret: quilling is also really easy to learn!

Quilling first caught my attention when I saw a framed quilled wedding invitation about 12 years ago. I was awed to discover that those delicate little flowers were actually strips of curled and molded paper. I immediately cut my own strips of paper and rolled them into teardrops. With a little glue, I had a beautiful flower ready for a handmade card. My feeling of satisfaction quickly turned to fascination, and all I could think was, "What else can I make?" Before long, I was creating original designs and eventually fashioning my own easy-to-use tools. As a result, quilling evolved from a hobby into a rewarding and inspiring career.

Quilling uses a few tools, paper strips, and glue. It's an inexpensive craft, where a little pack of paper truly goes a long way. The best part of quilling is its portability—take it with you from room to room or even in the car. Like many hobbies we turn to for enjoyment, quilling is a leisurely art that does take time. But the contemplative act of rolling paper is actually quite relaxing, and once you see the results—stunning works of art and impressive gifts—you may just find that you're hooked. I'm thrilled to share some new techniques and helpful tips I discovered while creating the projects for this book. From grouping petals to making spiral cut roses and peonies, these are versatile techniques that will add a whole new dimension to your quilling. My garden of 35 flowers offers blooms for all seasons and every occasion and creative inspiration for both beginning and experienced quillers. Get ready to have fun cultivating your own lovely quilled garden that will last a lifetime!

Quilling Basics

Growing a paper garden of stunning quilled flowers only requires some standard quilling tools and quilling paper in a variety of shades and colors. The techniques and various quilling shapes take only a little time to master.

MATERIALS

If you love paper crafting, jewelry making, or floral design, then you probably already have many of the supplies you'll need to make these projects.

PAPER

All of the projects in this book use quilling strips and/or text-weight paper. Some of the projects also call for colored cardstock.

Paper Strips

Precision-cut quilling papers are inexpensive and come in a variety of colors, lengths, widths, and weights. You'll find text-weight papers the easiest to roll, mold, and shape. The ⅛-inch (3 mm) width is usually the best for making quilled flowers because it's easy to combine shapes made with this width. Other popular quilling paper widths are ¼-inch (6 mm) and ¹⁄₁₆-inch (1.5 mm). You can cut your own paper strips, but for most flower designs, having exact paper widths will give you the best results and the most pleasing looking petals.

Text-weight paper

Text-weight paper comes in all different colors, and is either plain or patterned. The flower projects in this book work best with paper that's about the same thickness or weight of stationery paper or a greeting card envelope. It's easy to find text-weight paper at office supply, craft, or stationery stores.

EMBELLISHMENTS

Embellishments are a great way to add texture and style to your projects. A ribbon tied in a simple bow or tightly wrapped around the stem of a bouquet can give a project the perfect finishing touch. Pearls bring elegance to flowers, especially for formal occasions.

HOME DÉCOR ITEMS

Visit your favorite home store to find vases, frames, and boxes to display your quilled projects. Just like real flowers, your quilled creations will have depth and intricate beauty. Show them off in a vase or decorative pot, and they can serve as a centerpiece for your table. When you're going to place your flowers in a frame, look for shadow box frames that allow you to remove the glass—that way you can see the intricate details in the quilling without the glare of glass. And don't overlook the gift bags and boxes at such stores: Replace the usual bow on one with a beautiful quilled flower, and you'll add a much more personal touch to any gift.

CHALKS AND INKS

Because chalks and inkpads are perfect when you need a hint of color and depth, they are called for in many of the projects in this book. You can find them in the stamping section of your local art or craft store. A chalk applicator will allow you to apply chalk in the right places without getting it all over your work.

ADHESIVES

Always use white craft glue to make your quilled flowers. To adhere other materials, follow these simple guidelines: Use double-sided sticky tabs when adhering layers of cardstock together. Double-sided adhesive dots are useful when attaching embellishments such as pearls or ribbons to a particular spot. For jewelry, use a jewelry tacky glue to ensure that your quilling bonds to metal. Special glazes are great for gluing and adding a thin, protective coating over the quilling. Glue guns and glue sticks are perfect for securing floral wire stems to your quilled flowers and wooden wreaths.

JEWELRY SUPPLIES

Visit your local craft or beading store to find pendants, pin backs, hairclips, and other items to turn your quilled flowers into eye-catching accessories.

FLORAL SUPPLIES

To give your quilled flowers a sturdy stem, you'll need 18-gauge floral stem wire. A 22-gauge wire is thinner and more pliable. You can find floral wire in most craft stores.

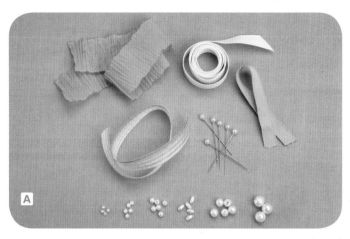

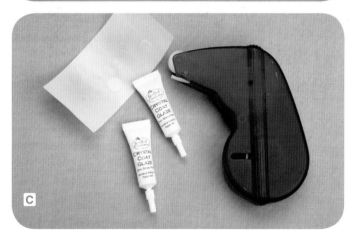

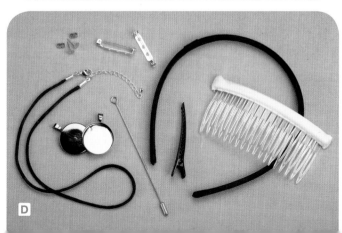

From top to bottom: **A** embellishment ribbons, pearls, and pins; **B** inkpads, chalks, and chalk applicator; **C** double-sided adhesive dots, double-sided sticky tabs, and adhesive glazes; **D** jewelry supplies

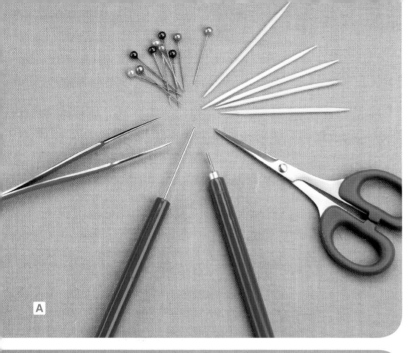

A

TOOLS

Special quilling tools designed to help you quickly roll your paper or sculpt your flower petals are inexpensive and can be found in local craft stores or online. The rest of the tools you need to make the projects in the book are easy to find, and many are quite likely already in your home.

Basic Quilling Toolbox

- Slotted tool
- Needle tool
- Fine-tipped tweezers
- Toothpicks
- Scissors
- Ruler
- Straight pins
- Corkboard or foam board
- Circle Template Board
- Combing Tool
- Grid Paper

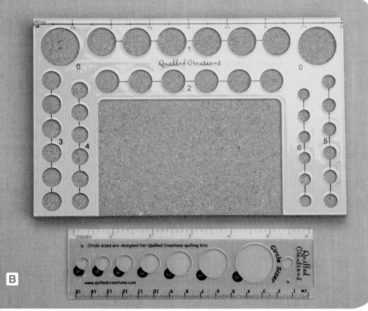

B

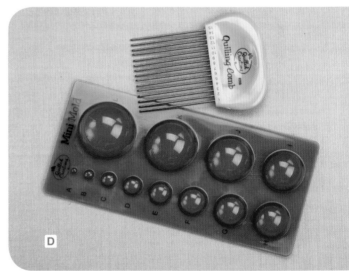

D

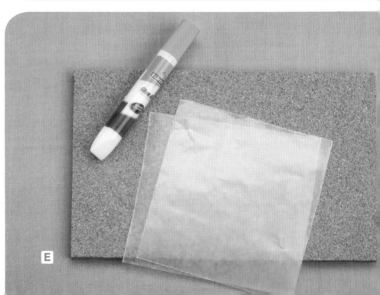

C

E

SLOTTED TOOL

The slotted tool has a narrow slot at the end of its needle that's designed to hold the quilling strip's end so it won't slip off when you start rolling the paper. It's perfect for beginners and for rolling quilled shapes such as the tight circle, grape roll, and cone.

NEEDLE TOOL

This is essentially a needle set into a handle. Because it doesn't have the slot to hold the strip's end, rolling paper with this tool takes a little more practice. Experienced quillers prefer using this tool because it leaves an attractive small, tight center. You can also use it to spread small amounts of glue on the paper strips.

FINE-TIPPED TWEEZERS

Tweezers with small, pointed tips are essential for quilling and for handling small pieces.

STRAIGHT PINS

Use straight pins to hold your quilled shapes together on a corkboard. Straight pins are also used to make off-center circles (page 13).

TOOTHPICKS

Toothpicks are useful for placing glue on the paper strips.

SCISSORS

Scissors with a fine tip are used for hand fringing, trimming, and cutting detailed shapes.

RULER

A ruler is helpful for measuring your paper strips to get the correct length.

CIRCLE TEMPLATE BOARD

This tool helps quickly size your coils and shapes so you can create symmetrical flowers with uniform petals easily. It's also useful when creating off-center circles (page 13).

CORKBOARD OR FOAM BOARD

These can be used to make off-center circles (page 13). (Cover these boards with waxed paper, so glued pieces won't stick to your work surface.)

GRID PAPER

Grid paper is used to align the pins when looping a strip of paper. It's placed on a corkboard or foam surface and covered with waxed paper.

COMBING TOOL

The combing tool forms a strip of paper into evenly spaced loops called wheatears (page 16). The numbered pins help track your looping pattern so that the process is fast and easy.

DOME-SHAPED MOLD

This product, available at craft stores or from online quilling stores, helps you shape tight circles into perfect domes. Flip it over, and you can use it to shape your flower petals into a cup shape. Small shallow round containers, such as very small cups or empty egg cartons can be used instead.

WAXED PAPER

Use this to cover your work surfaces so glued pieces won't stick.

CRAFT GLUE

Since you're gluing paper to paper, you only need small dabs of glue to hold your coils together. Choose a liquid or water-based glue that dries clear. Avoid overly tacky glues that are hard to remove from your fingers and tools—these can slow you down and ruin your quilled shapes.

PAPER TRIMMER

A paper trimmer can make straight-line cuts quickly for your cards or background pieces.

CRAFT KNIFE AND CUTTING MAT

These are handy tools to use when cutting and trimming thick paper sticks (such as those made with the Trellis Stick technique [page 15]).

WIRE CUTTERS

Use wire cutters to cut floral wire to length.

NEEDLE-NOSE PLIERS

The round, tapered tips of needle-nose pliers make them ideal for shaping floral wire into small loops, which is needed in the Adding a Stem technique (page 14).

On opposite page: A clockwise from top: straight pins, toothpicks, scissors, slotted tool, needle tool, and fine-tipped tweezers; B circle template board and ruler; C grid paper and cork board; D combing tool and dome-shaped mold; E waxed paper and craft glue

TECHNIQUES

It's always fascinating to see how many different ways a single strip of paper can be shaped. Once you've perfected the basics of rolling, you'll see how fun and simple it is to do the rest!

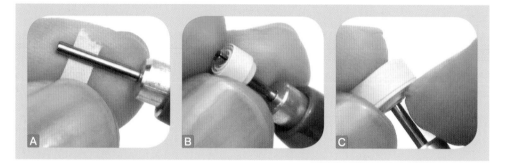

tip

Tear quilling strips to the specified length instead of cutting them. The torn feathered ends leave a less obvious seam once they're glued.

ROLLING WITH A SLOTTED TOOL

1. Insert the end of the paper into the slot from the top. **A**

2. Begin rolling the paper strip around the tip by rotating the tool in one direction (it doesn't matter which direction you rotate it). **B**

3. To keep the coil's center from being pulled out, remove the coil by pushing from behind or underneath the coil instead of pulling it off. **C**

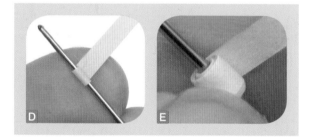

ROLLING WITH A NEEDLE TOOL

1. Scratch the end of the paper with your nail to soften the paper fibers. This will make it easier to wrap the paper end around the needle tip. You can also moisten the end of the paper strip so that it sticks to the needle when you're ready to roll it. **D**

2. To start the roll, squeeze the end of the paper around the needle, and roll it between your fingers without rotating the needle tool. The roll will start forming once the paper end is tucked under itself. **E**

3. Continue to use light pressure, rolling the paper around the needle tool by moving your thumb and finger in opposite directions.

4. Slide the coil off the needle tool.

ATTACHING END-TO-END

Overlap the ends of two paper strips and glue them together. Roll the paper strip. **F** and **G**

ROLLING MULTIPLE STRIPS

For added color and dimension, stack and glue two paper strips together. Then roll both paper strips at the same time. **H** and **I**

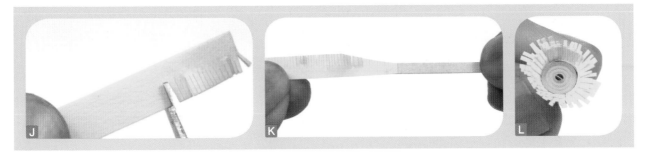

FRINGING

1. To begin, fold the paper in half lengthwise. Starting at the fold, cut slits into the paper. **J**

2. Unfold the paper strip and make an additional slit at the fold. If called for in the project, trim the fringes at an angle. **K**

3. Roll the fringed strip into a tight circle. Fluff the fringes outward.

GLUING SHAPES TO A BACKGROUND

1. Create a puddle of glue on a small notepad or other surface.

2. Use tweezers to pick up your quilled piece and place it in the glue. **M**

3. Gently tap off the excess glue on the notepad, and position the quilled piece on the background.

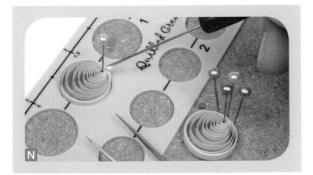

MAKING AN OFF-CENTER CIRCLE

Roll a loose circle and place it on a corkboard or in a circle template board. Pin the center of the coil to one side. Use tweezers to even out the coils. Spread a thin layer of glue over the paper edges between the pins, and let it dry. **N**

For a fringed flower with a center, glue a strip of paper to the end of the fringed paper strip before rolling. Starting at the unfringed end, roll the strips into a tight circle and fluff the fringes outward. **L**

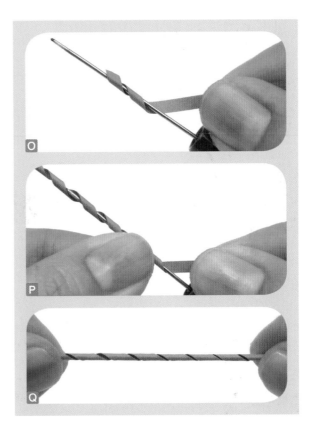

MAKING SPIRALS

1. Using a ⅛-inch (3 mm) strip of paper, wrap the end of the paper strip around the needle tool at a 45° angle from the handle. **O**

2. Roll the paper strip up the needle with your thumb and finger without rotating the needle tool. **P**

3. Remove the spiral from the tool. While holding both ends of the spiral, twist and pull the spiral tighter to even out the coils. **Q**

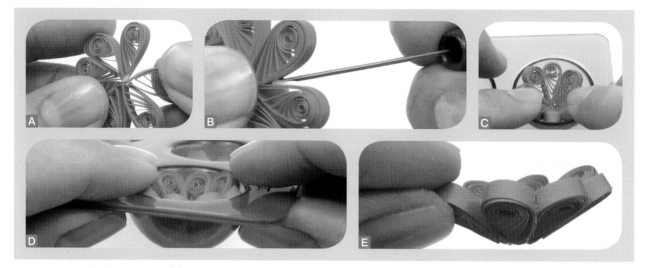

CUPPING PETALS

1. Glue each petal together at the center point. Let them dry. **A**

2. Spread glue between each petal. **B**

3. Place your flower inside a dome-shaped mold, small cup, or egg carton cup. **C**

4. Press down and hold it in the cup for a few minutes. **D**

5. When the glue is dry, remove the flower, and it will hold its cup shape. **E**

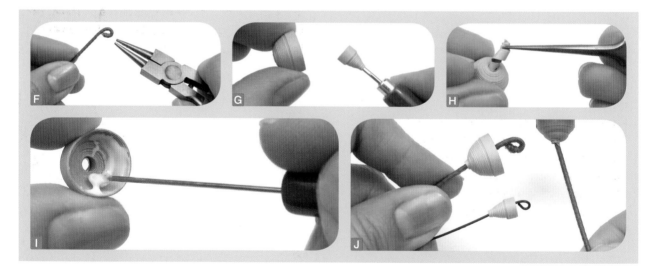

ADDING A STEM

1. Cut the wire to the appropriate length with wire cutters. Use needle-nose pliers to bend a small loop at one end. **F**

2. With strips of paper, roll a grape roll or cone for the flower's calyx (page 18). **G**

3. If the hole isn't big enough for the stem wire, use tweezers to pull out and trim off a few coils from the center of the grape roll. **H**

4. Spread glue on the inside of the quilled calyx and let it dry. **I**

5. Insert the wire into the calyx and glue the stem to the flower. **J**

SUPPORTING PETAL COILS

To keep the coils in your leaves and petals from falling out or unraveling, spread glue on the back side of the construction. **K**

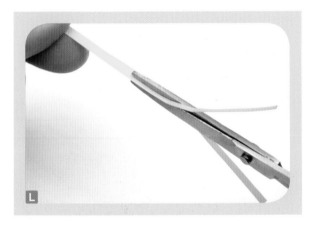

CUTTING NARROW STRIPS
(¹⁄₁₆ INCH [1.6 MM])

To cut a ⅛-inch (3 mm) wide strip of paper in half, use fine-tip scissors. Hold a paper strip in one hand and the scissors in the other hand, and watch the tip of the scissors, not the scissor blades, as you cut toward the center of the strip. By watching the scissors' tip, you will guide the cutting direction and always cut down the middle. **L**

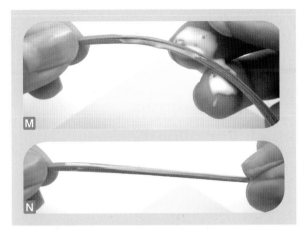

MAKING TRELLIS STICKS

1. Trellis sticks are made with 10 strips of full-length quilling paper stacked and glued together: Stack 10 strips into a neat pile to form one thick stick. Place a puddle of craft glue on a small notepad. Dip your thumb and fingers in the glue and spread it onto all four sides of the stacked paper strips in small sections. **M**

2. As you spread the glue along the stack of strips, press the strips together to keep them as one straight, thick stick. Continue spreading the glue and pressing the strip together on all sides until the entire length is covered. Let it dry completely. Cut the sticks to the length(s) specified in the project. **N**

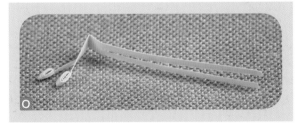

MAKING STAMENS

1. Fold a strip of paper in half lengthwise.

2. Cut the folded strip down the middle lengthwise, stopping just before the fold.

3. Unfold the paper strip to reveal four thin strips that are attached and meet at the center fold.

4. Roll the outer end of each of the four thin strips into a tight circle.

5. Pinch each tight circle flat, creating four stamens. **O**

LOOPING BY COMBING

A combing tool has a handle with numbered prongs that allow you to make evenly spaced loops quickly and easily.

1. Make a small fold in the paper strip at the top prong (prong #1). Place glue at the fold. Wrap the strip of paper around prong #2 and back up around prong #1.

2. Wrap the paper around prong #3 and then back around prong #1, then prong #4 and back up to #1, etc. Glue after each loop. E

WRAPPING MULTIPLE QUILLED PIECES

Glue the quilled pieces together to form a rough petal shape. Glue a strip of paper to the base, and then wrap the strip tightly around the quilled pieces. Squeeze and re-pinch points if necessary to create a petal of a specific shape. A and B

LOOPING BY HUSKING

Place waxed paper or a clear plastic bag over grid paper (this will keep glue from sticking to the paper).

1. Glue a small loop at the end of a paper strip. Place a pin inside the loop and secure it on the grid paper. F

2. Insert another pin in the grid and wrap the strip around the pin. G

3. Continue looping and gluing after each loop. Remove the pins to release the wheatear. H

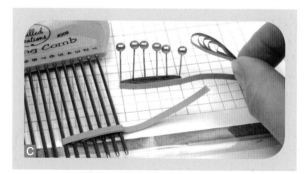

LOOPING

There are three methods to looping, which is also known as creating wheatears: combing, husking, and by hand. The combing tool makes evenly spaced loops very quickly, but if you don't have a combing tool, you can do the looping technique by using pins and grid paper (husking) or simply by hand. C

LOOPING BY HAND

1. Make a small loop with the paper strip. Wrap the paper around the end, and make another loop that is slightly larger. I

2. Continue making larger loops until you've reached the instructed size. (It's not necessary to glue after each loop for this method.)

CREATING A SPIRAL ROSE

Whether you hand cut your spirals or buy them as die-cuts, this technique is simply amazing. The beauty of spiral roses is how quickly the rose begins to "bloom" as you start rolling your paper strip! Vary the look of your roses by using chalk and inkpads for embellishment. **J**

1. Trace the spiral pattern onto your paper. **K**

2. For the smaller spirals, cut a random wavy pattern on the spiral line. For the larger spiral, cut along the spiral line. Then use scissors to cut the grooves along the outer spiral edge. **L**

3. Carefully crumple the spiral into a ball to add texture and creases to your petals. **M**

4. Flatten and reshape the paper into a spiral and start rolling at the outer end of the spiral. Roll with gentle finger pressure. The coils will not sit flat, but will instead start blooming open at one edge. When you've reached the spiral's center, remove the coil from the quilling tool and let it unravel. **N**

5. Shape the rose into the desired size; then turn the rose over, spread glue on the spiral's center, and press it into the coils. **O**

It's fun experimenting with the spiral pattern and varying the petal cuttings. Try fringing the outer end of the spiral and adding chalk to create a different look. Or, after reshaping a crumpled spiral, rub ink on the edges to add color and texture. **P** and **Q**

USING THE TEMPLATES

The project instructions in this book refer to Templates that depict how to assemble the separate quilled shapes composing each flower. The Templates also include diagrams of each finished flower, allowing you to arrange your paper blossoms right there on the page. All of the Templates and diagrams showing the finished flowers are depicted at actual size.

BASIC QUILLED SHAPES

TIGHT CIRCLE

Roll the paper strip until you reach the end. Glue the end to the roll without letting the coil expand open.

LOOSE CIRCLE

Roll the paper strip as you did for the tight circle. Remove the coil from the tool and let it unravel open. Spread a small dab of glue on the loose end, and press it against the coil.

OFF-CENTER CIRCLE

Place the loose coil on a corkboard or in a circle template board, and pin the center of the coil to one side. Use tweezers to even out the coils. Spread a thin layer of glue over the paper edges between the pins, and let it dry.

TEARDROP

Roll a loose circle and simply pinch a point on the coil. To evenly pinch each coil layer, shift the center of the coil to one side and then pinch a point.

MARQUISE

Starting with a loose circle, use both hands to pinch points at opposite sides of the circle at the same time.

HALF CIRCLE

Start with a teardrop. Pinch a second point to create one rounded side and one flat side.

CRESCENT

Start with a teardrop. Pinch a second point to create a half circle, then curve the two points gently toward each other.

TRIANGLE

Start with a teardrop. Press the rounded end inward to form two additional points.

HEART

Holding the point of a teardrop, use your finger to press in on the rounded end.

TIGHT/LOOSE CIRCLE

Roll the paper strip into a tight circle. Remove it from the tool and let it slightly expand open between your fingers. Spread a small dab of glue on the loose end and press it against the coil. This shape can be pinched into a teardrop or marquise.

GRAPE ROLL

Roll a tight circle. Shape it into a dome using a small round surface or a dome-shaped mold. Spread glue on the inside or outside to hold its shape. This shape can be pinched into a teardrop or marquise.

CONE

Roll a strip of paper on a slight angle. Glue the end of the strip to the roll without letting the coil expand open.

BASIC QUILLED SCROLLS

LOOSE SCROLL

Roll a paper strip at one end, and leave the other end loose or unglued.

SWOOPING SCROLL

Roll a loose scroll, and then unravel part of the scroll. Gently re-roll the scroll, making the coils farther apart.

DOUBLE SCROLL

Fold the strip of paper in half. Starting from the fold, roll the paper strip into a swooping scroll. Shift one layer of the paper slightly and glue the loose ends together.

Just a Pinch—Curving Points

You can make just about any shape from a loose circle by pinching a point or points. Curving points on a quilled shape gives you even more shaping options. Use your fingers or the tip of the quilling tool to curve points. Pinch a point on the glued paper end to hide the seam.

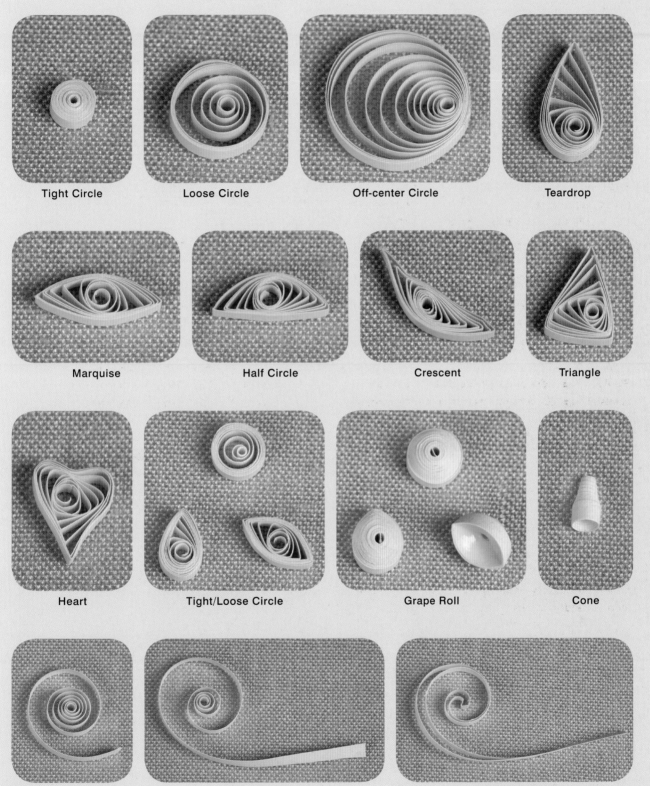

Tight Circle

Loose Circle

Off-center Circle

Teardrop

Marquise

Half Circle

Crescent

Triangle

Heart

Tight/Loose Circle

Grape Roll

Cone

Loose Scroll

Swooping Scroll

Double Scroll

Projects FOR A PAPER GARDEN

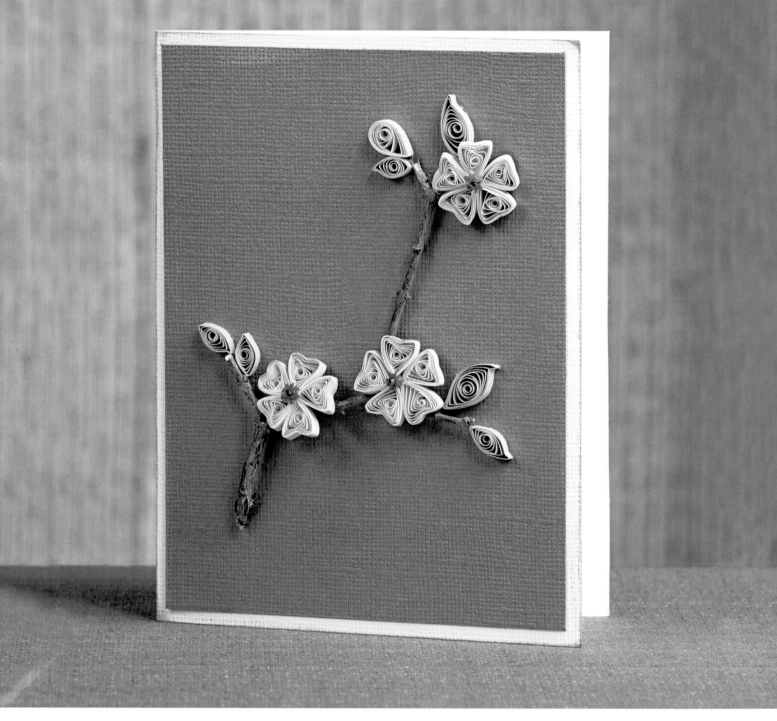

Cherry Blossom CARD

Celebrate springtime with these pretty pink blossoms, which are perfect for Mother's Day. Add real branches to bring life to your quilled card.

WHAT YOU NEED

- Templates (page 24)
- Basic Quilling Toolbox (page 10)
- Cardstock: off-white and brown
- ⅛-inch (3 mm) quilling paper: pale pink, dark red, and moss green
- Brown inkpad
- Double-sided adhesive dots
- Small pieces of branches

QUILLING SHAPES Tight/loose coil   Heart Tight/loose teardrop Marquise

WHAT YOU DO

1. To make the card base, cut an 8½ x 5¼-inch (21.6 x 13.5 cm) rectangle from the off-white cardstock. Score and fold in half to make a 4¼ x 5¼-inch (10.8 x 13.5 cm) card.

2. Cut a 4 x 5-inch (10 x 12.7 cm) rectangle from the brown cardstock. Ink the edges of the card with the brown ink.

3. To make each cherry blossom, roll five 8-inch (20.3 cm) lengths of the pale pink quilling paper into tight/loose coils. Pinch them into hearts. Glue five petals together to form a blossom. Make three of these.

4. To make each blossom's center, use a 3-inch (7.6 cm) length of the dark red quilling paper. Fringe the entire length of paper (page 13). Cut into three 1-inch (2.5 cm) lengths. Roll each length into a fringed flower. Glue each to the center of one cherry blossom.

5. To make the bud, roll an 8-inch (20.3 cm) length of pale pink into a tight/loose teardrop.

6. To make the leaves, roll two 8-inch (20.3 cm) lengths and four 4-inch (10 cm) lengths of the moss green quilling paper into curved marquises.

7. Attach the branches to the card front with the double-sided adhesive dots.

8. Glue the cherry blossoms, bud, and leaves to the card.

Petal

Center

Large Leaf

Small Leaf

Cherry Blossom
assembled at actual size

Iris TRELLIS SUNCATCHER

The iris takes its name from the Greek word for rainbow.
The intricacies of this flower's purples and yellows sit center
stage when it catches the sunlight of a brightly lit window.

WHAT YOU NEED

- Templates (page 27)
- Basic Quilling Toolbox (page 10)
- ⅛-inch (3 mm) quilling paper: purple, pale yellow, dark purple, mint green, green, and pumpkin
- ¼-inch (6 mm) quilling paper: black
- Craft knife
- String

QUILLING SHAPES   Teardrop    Half circle   Off-center circle

WHAT YOU DO

1. To make the small petals, roll three 8-inch (20.3 cm) lengths of the purple quilling paper into loose circles. Shape one into a teardrop and the other two into half circles.

2. To make the large petals, tear a 4-inch (10 cm) length of the pale yellow quilling paper and a 16-inch (40.6 cm) length of the purple quilling paper. Glue the strips together using the attaching end-to-end technique (page 12). Starting from the pale yellow end, roll the strip into an off-center loose circle (page 13). Wrap a strip of the dark purple quilling paper around the petal three times. Shape it into an oval. Make three large petals and glue them together, and then glue the small petals to the large petals, using the photo for placement.

3. For the leaves, layer and glue a 16-inch (40.6 cm) length of the mint green quilling paper and a 16-inch (40.6 cm) length of the green quilling paper together

at one end. Loop the entire length of paper and trim off any excess paper (page 16). Make two leaves.

4. For the trellis, use ten 16-inch (40.6 cm) lengths of the pumpkin quilling paper and glue them together using the trellis stick technique (page 15). Repeat to make another 16-inch- (40.6 cm) length pumpkin trellis stick. Cut these into three 5-inch (12.7 cm) sticks and seven 2-inch (5 cm) sticks. Using the photo or template for reference, glue them together in a grid pattern.

5. For the frame, use ten 16-inch (40.6 cm) lengths of the black quilling paper and glue them together using the trellis stick technique. Cut the stick into four pieces to fit around the trellis, and then glue the pieces to the trellis. Wrap and glue another black strip around the entire frame.

6. Insert the string for hanging your suncatcher at the top and tie a knot.

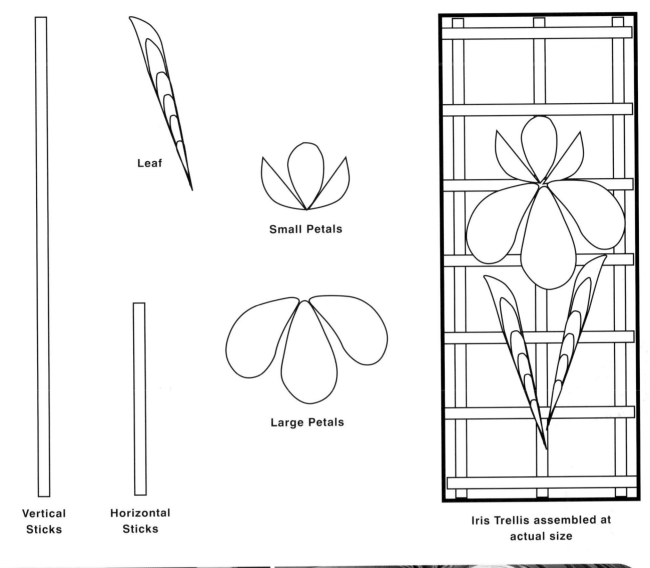

Leaf

Small Petals

Large Petals

Vertical
Sticks

Horizontal
Sticks

Iris Trellis assembled at
actual size

Daisy PENDANT NECKLACE

Want to show your family and friends the beauty of paper quilling? Just quill this simple daisy and place it in a pendant to create eye-catching wearable art!

WHAT YOU NEED

- Templates (page 29)
- Basic Quilling Toolbox (page 10)

- ⅛-inch (3 mm) quilling paper: white, light yellow, and dark yellow
- Jewelry glaze (clear)

- 1-inch- (2.5 cm) diameter round pendant blank
- Satin cording

QUILLING SHAPES   Circle   Off-center circle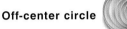

WHAT YOU DO

1. For the petals, roll eight 4-inch (10 cm) lengths of the white quilling paper into loose circles. Shape them into off-center circles (page 13). Pinch the off-center portion to make an oval shape.

2. For the center, stack and glue a 2-inch (5 cm) length of the light yellow and a 2-inch (5 cm) length of the dark yellow quilling paper together. Roll them into a loose circle (page 12).

3. Spread a thin layer of jewelry glaze at the bottom of the pendant blank. Place the petals and center into the pendant.

4. Add the satin cording to the pendant.

Petal

Center

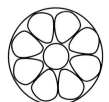

Daisy Pendant assembled at actual size

tip

To give your piece a polished look, add another layer of glaze on top after the flower has dried.

FRAMED Sunflower

You are my sunshine! This sunflower, full of layers, dimension, and texture, will make you happy even when skies are gray.

WHAT YOU NEED

- Templates (page 32)
- Basic Quilling Toolbox (page 10)
- Cardstock: black and brown
- 2-inch (5 cm) circle template
- Pencil
- ⅛-inch (3 mm) quilling paper: yellow, moss green, and brown
- Orange and green chalk
- Chalk applicator
- Dome-shaped mold
- 8 x 10-inch (20.3 x 25.4 cm) shadow box frame and mat

QUILLING SHAPES   Half Circle   Grape Roll   Tight Circle ⊙   Marquise

WHAT YOU DO

1. Cut an 8 x 10-inch (20.3 x 25.4 cm) piece of the black cardstock for the base.

2. Trace and cut a circle that's 2 inches (5 cm) in diameter from the brown cardstock.

3. For the sunflower petals, roll two 16-inch (40.6 cm) lengths of the yellow quilling paper into flat half circles and glue them together. Wrap each petal three times with a yellow strip (see Template Ⓐ). Make 25 petals. Chalk each petal's base with the orange chalk.

4. For the sunflower center, roll seven 8-inch (20.3 cm) lengths of the moss green quilling paper into grape rolls. Roll thirty 8-inch (20.3 cm) lengths of the brown quilling paper into grape rolls. Glue the moss green and brown grape rolls to the brown cardstock. Use scissors to make a wavy cut around the grape rolls. Chalk the moss green grape rolls with the green chalk.

5. To raise the sunflower's center, roll three 16-inch (40.6 cm) lengths of brown quilling paper into tight circles. Glue them to the back of the flower's center.

6. Glue 16 petals around and to the sunflower's center, adhering them just beneath the outer edge of the brown cardstock circle. Layer and glue the remaining petals on top of the previous petals (see Template Ⓑ).

7. For the small leaf, roll five 16-inch (40.6 cm) lengths of moss green into marquises and glue together. Wrap twice with a moss green strip (see Template Ⓒ). For the large leaf, roll seven 16-inch (40.6 cm) lengths of moss green into marquises and glue them together. Wrap twice with a moss green strip (see Template Ⓓ). Rub green chalk around the leaves.

8. Glue the leaves to the black cardstock, and then place the quilled flower into a matted shadow box frame.

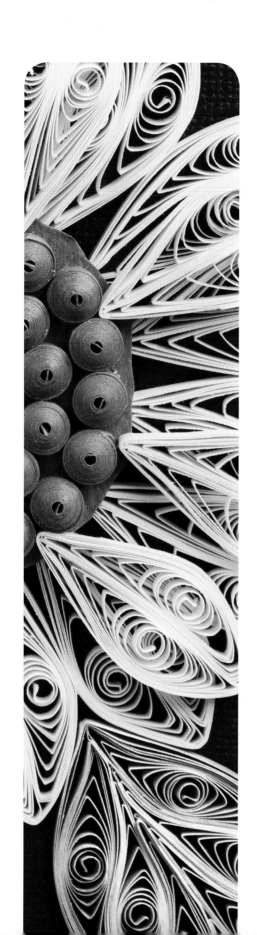

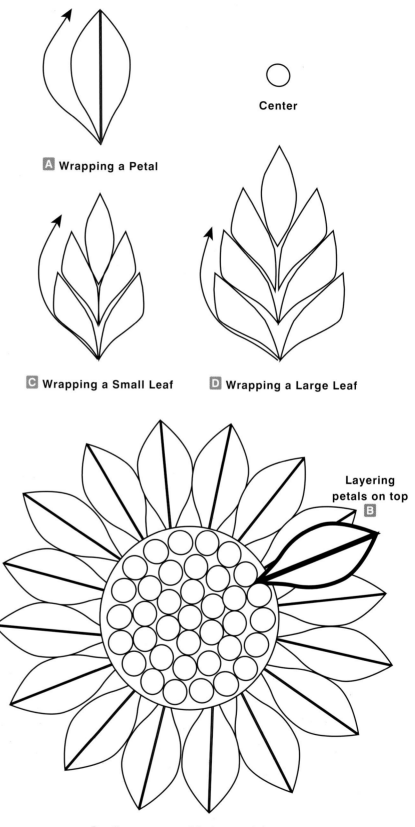

Center

A Wrapping a Petal

C Wrapping a Small Leaf   D Wrapping a Large Leaf

Layering
petals on top
B

Sunflower assembled at actual size

Poppy

Sometimes a single bloom makes the biggest impression.
The intricate details and graceful petals of this poppy
make this a sure conversation starter for your table.

WHAT YOU NEED

- Templates (page 35)
- Basic Quilling Toolbox (page 10)
- ⅛-inch (3 mm) quilling paper: red, forest green, moss green, and black
- ¼-inch (6 mm) quilling paper: black
- Dome-shaped mold
- Floral wire (18 gauge)
- Vase

QUILLING SHAPES   Marquise 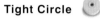   Tight Circle

WHAT YOU DO

1. For each petal, roll twelve 8-inch (20.3 cm) lengths of the red quilling paper into marquises. Wrap six marquises three times with a red strip (page 16 [see Template A]). While wrapping, squeeze the marquises flat or re-pinch points if necessary. Glue two wrapped marquises together to make a petal. Spread glue on the back side (page 15). Make six petals.

2. For the calyx, glue three 16-inch (40.6 cm) lengths of the forest green quilling paper together using the attaching end-to-end technique (page 12). Roll this strip into a tight circle. Shape it into a shallow dome and spread glue on the inside.

3. Glue three petals to the calyx for the bottom layer. Glue three other petals on top.

4. Make a small loop at the end of a floral wire. Insert it between the petals and through the calyx, and secure it with glue.

5. To make the center, cut one 8-inch (20.3 cm) length of the moss green and one 8-inch (20.3 cm) length of the ⅛-inch (3 mm) black quilling paper. Glue the moss green strip to the black strip using the attaching end-to-end technique. Cut a 4-inch (10 cm) length of the ¼-inch (6 mm) black quilling paper, and fringe it (page 13). Glue the moss green and black strip to the fringed black strip (black ends together) using the end-to-end technique (see Template B). Starting from the moss green end, roll the entire strip into a tight circle. Curl the fringes outward. Glue the center to the petals.

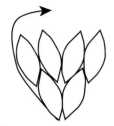

A Wrapping a Half Petal

Two Wrapped
Half Petals Together

Poppy assembled at actual size

(not to scale)

B Joining the fringed Center

Orchid PIN

36

Delicate, exotic, and graceful orchids are one of the most coveted flowers in the world. Why not make one that will accessorize your wardrobe and last forever even if you don't have a green thumb?

WHAT YOU NEED

■ **Templates (page 38)**

■ **Basic Quilling Toolbox (page 10)**

■ **⅛-inch (3 mm) quilling paper: light purple, purple, and pale yellow**

■ **Purple chalk**

■ **Chalk applicator**

■ **Stickpin**

■ **Jewelry tacky glue**

QUILLING SHAPES   Marquise   Crescent   Grape Roll

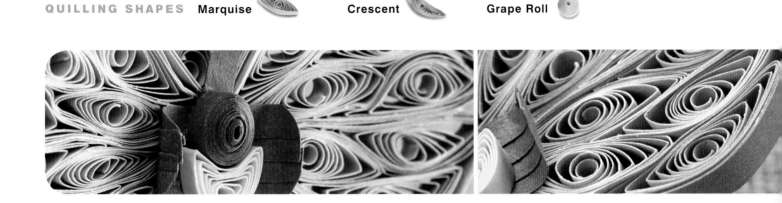

WHAT YOU DO

1. For each large petal, roll ten 8-inch (20.3 cm) lengths of the light purple quilling paper into loose circles. Pinch these into four marquises and six half circles. To begin making one half petal, glue two of the marquises to three of the half circles, making sure the half circles all face the same direction, as shown in Template **A**. Wrap a light purple strip around the construction three times (page 16 [see Template **A**]). While wrapping, squeeze the pieces flat or re-pinch points if necessary. Make another half petal with the remaining marquises and half circles. Glue the two wrapped half petals together to make one large petal. Chalk the edges with purple chalk. Spread glue on the back side (supporting petal coils, page 15). Make two large petals.

2. For each small petal, roll five 8-inch (20.3 cm) lengths of light purple into marquises. Arrange these as shown in Template **B**, and glue together. Wrap a light purple strip around it three times to form a marquise-shaped petal (see Template **B**). While wrapping, squeeze the marquises flat or re-pinch their points if necessary. Chalk the edges with purple chalk. Spread glue on the back side. Make three of these small marquise-shaped petals.

3. Glue the three small petals together. Glue the two large petals on top.

4. Using the photo and Templates for reference, make the following pieces for the orchid's center:

● Cut a ½-inch (1.3 cm) length of the purple quilling paper and round one end.

● Roll an 8-inch (20.3 cm) length of the purple quilling paper into a grape roll and glue inside to hold the shape.

● Glue four 1-inch (2.5 cm) lengths of purple side-to-side by overlapping slightly. Round the corners and curl into a "C" shape.

● Roll a 4-inch (10 cm) length of pale yellow into a crescent.

● Roll two 8-inch (20.3 cm) lengths of purple into curved marquises.

5. Glue all of the center pieces together and secure them to the flower.

6. Attach the stickpin to the back of the orchid with the jewelry tacky glue.

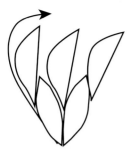

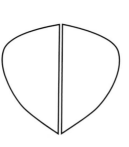

A Wrapping Half of a Large Petal

Two wrapped Half Petals as a Large Petal

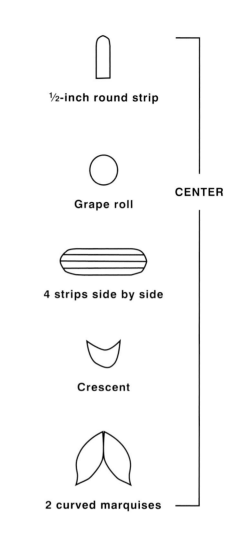

½-inch round strip

Grape roll

4 strips side by side

Crescent

2 curved marquises

CENTER

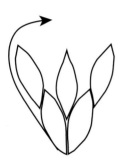

B Wrapping a Small Petal

Wrapped Small Petal

Orchid assembled at actual size

ORCHID VARIATION

Create a variation of the orchid in white with two blossoms and floral wire stems (page 14). Glue two large marquise grape rolls together to create the bud.

FRAMED Fuchsias & Hummingbird

40

Beautiful, delicate fuchsias droop delightfully in this
framed arrangement. The vibrant blossoms are great
for attracting hummingbirds!

WHAT YOU NEED

- **Templates (page 42)**
- **Basic Quilling Toolbox (page 10)**
- **1/8-inch (3 mm) quilling paper:** fuchsia, raspberry, green, teal, ivory, and red
- **Text-weight paper: purple**
- **Floral wire (22 gauge)**
- **Shadow box frame**

QUILLING SHAPES   **Teardrop**   **Tight/loose circle**   **Grape roll**   **Half circle**

Triangle   **Off-center circle**

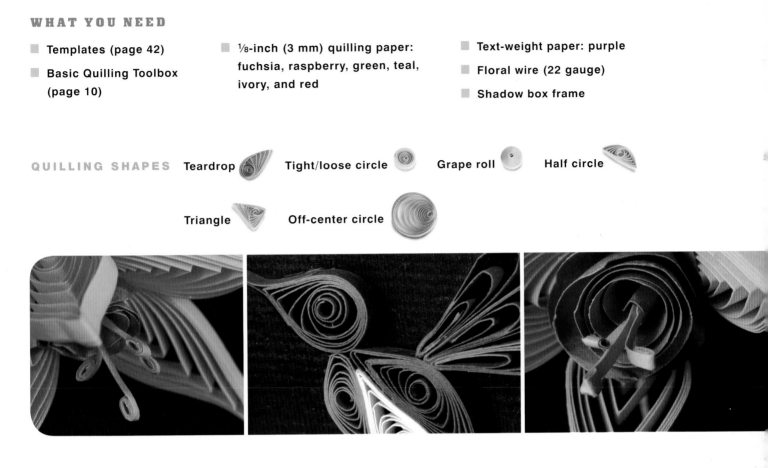

WHAT YOU DO

1. For the outer petals of the fuchsia flowers, roll twelve 16-inch (40.6 cm) lengths of the fuchsia quilling paper into off-center circles (page 13). Pinch each shape into a long teardrop. For the inner petals, cut a 2-inch (5 cm) square piece of the purple text-weight paper into a spiral and roll it into a spiral rose (page 17). Make three of these. Glue four of the outer petals around each purple rose to make three flowers.

2. For each flower center, use a 2-inch (5 cm) length of the raspberry quilling paper and follow the making stamens technique (page 15). Make three flower centers, and glue each to a flower.

3. For each fuchsia bud, roll a 16-inch (40.6 cm) length of fuchsia into a tight/loose circle. Pinch into a curved teardrop.

4. For the calyx, roll five 8-inch (20.3 cm) lengths of fuchsia into grape rolls. Attach a wire stem with a loop inside each grape roll, and glue it to the flowers and buds (page 14). Wrap the stems with the green quilling paper.

5. For the leaves, roll ten 16-inch (40.6 cm) lengths of green into teardrops. Glue two together to make a leaf. Make five leaves.

6. To make the hummingbird head, roll a 4-inch (10 cm) length of the teal quilling paper into a teardrop. Fold a 2-inch (5 cm) length of teal in half and glue it to the teardrop's point for the beak. For the body, roll an 8-inch (20.3 cm) length of teal and an 8-inch (20.3 cm) length of the ivory quilling paper into half circles and glue them together. To make the red breast, roll a 4-inch (10 cm) length of the red quilling paper into a half circle and glue it to the body. For the tail, roll a 6-inch (15 cm) length of teal into a triangle and glue it to the body. For the wings, make one 3-looped piece and two 4-looped pieces from teal strips (page 16). Glue them together and pinch the base flat. Glue it to the body.

7. Glue the flowers, leaves, and hummingbird to the frame.

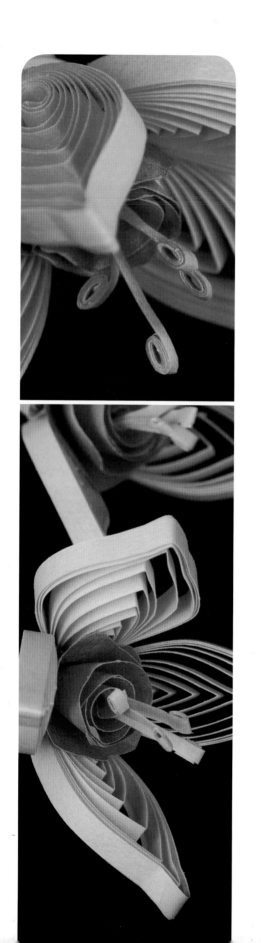

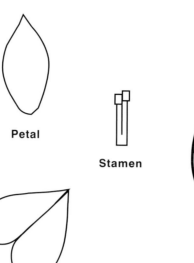

Petal

Stamen

Leaf

2-inch (5 cm) spiral

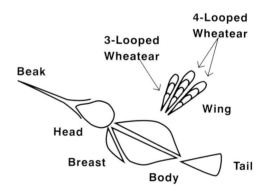

4-Looped Wheatear

3-Looped Wheatear

Beak

Head

Wing

Breast

Body

Tail

Hummingbird assembled at actual size

Fuchsia assembled at actual size

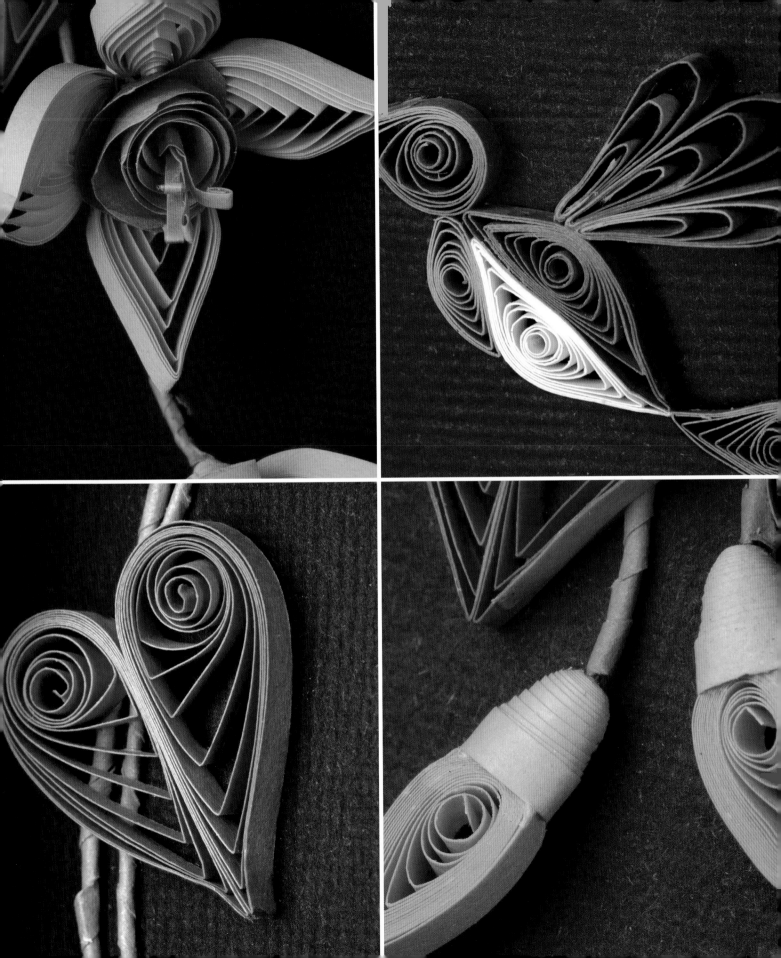

Zinnia GIFT BOWS

Why use a bow when you can dress up a gift box with a quilled zinnia! Off-centered petals and the cupping technique give these flowers full-bloom beauty.

WHAT YOU NEED

- Templates (page 46)
- Basic Quilling Toolbox (page 10)
- ⅛-inch (3 mm) quilling paper: orange, dark red, pink, fuchsia, yellow, moss green
- ¼-inch (6 mm) quilling paper: yellow
- Circle template board
- Dome-shaped mold (or shallow round container)

QUILLING SHAPES   Off-center circle   Teardrop

WHAT YOU DO

1. For the orange zinnia, make uniform-size petals with a circle template board. Roll with the orange quilling paper each of the following layers:

   Layer 1 – Roll ten 16-inch (40.6 cm) strips into loose circles, each with a ¾-inch (2 cm) diameter.

   Layer 2 – Roll ten 16-inch (40.6 cm) strips into loose circles, each with a ¾-inch (2 cm) diameter.

   Layer 3 – Roll eight 12-inch (30.5 cm) strips into loose circles, each with a ⅝-inch (1.6 cm) diameter.

   Layer 4 – Roll eight 8-inch (20.3 cm) strips into loose circles, each with a ½-inch (1.3 cm) diameter.

2. Form each loose circle into an off-center circle (page 13) and then pinch into a long teardrop. (Note: Gluing the loose circle coils into off-center circles will prevent each coil's center from falling out.)

3. Glue the layer 1 teardrops together so they lie flat.

4. Glue layers 2, 3, and 4 together using the cupping technique (page 14).

5. Stack and glue the layers together.

6. For the center, cut a 2-inch (5 cm) length of the yellow quilling paper and fringe it (page 13). Measure an 8-inch (20.3 cm) length of the dark red quilling paper. Glue the two strips together using the attaching end-to-end technique (page 12). Starting from the crimson end, roll it into a tight circle. Curl the fringes outward and glue the center to the flower.

7. Repeat this process for the pink and yellow zinnias.

Layer 1 & 2

Layer 3

Layer 4

Center (not to scale)

Zinnia assembled at actual size

Lily HEADBAND & BARRETTE

You can use quilling to make fun hair accessories that take the paper art to a whole new level. These delightful lilies will accent any hairstyle.

WHAT YOU NEED

- Templates (page 49)
- Basic Quilling Toolbox (page 10)
- ⅛-inch (3 mm) quilling paper: white and yellow
- Dome-shaped mold or shallow round container
- Green and yellow chalk
- Chalk applicator
- Glue gun with glue sticks
- Headband
- Barrette

QUILLING SHAPE   Half circle

WHAT YOU DO

1. To make each petal, roll two 16-inch (40.6 cm) lengths of the white quilling paper into half circles. Glue them together, using the template for reference. Make six petals and glue them together in groups of three. Shape one group of petals using the cupping technique (page 14). Stack the two groups of petals as shown in the template, and glue them together. Make two flowers.

2. Chalk the center of each lily with green and yellow chalk.

3. To make the stamens, cut a 4-inch (10 cm) length of the yellow quilling paper, and follow the making stamens technique (page 15). Glue it to one flower. Repeat to make another set of stamens, and glue it to the second lily.

4. Use the glue gun to attach one lily to the headband and the other to the barrette.

Petal

Stamens

Lily assembled at actual size

Dogwood & Bird's Nest WREATH

50

Welcome the arrival of warm weather with a little spring wreath.
Hidden within the blossoms is a nest holding precious eggs.

WHAT YOU NEED

- Templates (page 52)
- Basic Quilling Toolbox (page 10)
- ⅛-inch (3 mm) quilling paper: white, forest green, brown, light brown, and light blue
- ¼-inch (6 mm) quilling paper: moss green
- Vine wreath, 6 inches (15.2 cm) in diameter
- Brown and yellow chalk
- Chalk applicator
- Glue gun with glue sticks

QUILLING SHAPES **Half circle**   **Teardrop**   **Grape roll**

WHAT YOU DO

1. For each dogwood petal, roll eight 8-inch (20.3 cm) lengths of the white quilling paper into half circles. Glue them in pairs to make a 4-petal flower. Chalk the tips of the petals with brown chalk. Make 12 flowers.

2. For each flower center, fringe a 1-inch (2.5 cm) length of the moss green quilling paper, and roll it into a tight circle (page 13). Chalk the fringes with yellow chalk. Make 12 fringed centers and glue one to each flower.

3. For each leaf, roll two 16-inch (40.6 cm) lengths of the forest green quilling paper into teardrops and glue them together. Make smaller leaves with 8-inch (20.3 cm) and 12-inch (30.5 cm) lengths of forest green. Make 20 leaves in all.

4. For the bird's nest, roll three 16-inch (40.6 cm) lengths of the brown and three 16-inch (40.6 cm) lengths of the light brown quilling paper into spirals (page 13). Twist and coil them together to form a nest and use the glue gun to hold the nest's shape.

5. To make the eggs, glue two 16-inch (40.6 cm) lengths of the light blue quilling paper together using the attaching end-to-end technique (page 12). Roll the resulting 32-inch (81.3 cm) length of paper into a grape roll, and then shape it into an oval to form an egg. Make three eggs and use the glue gun to secure them inside the nest.

6. Use the glue gun to attach the flowers, leaves, and nest to the wreath.

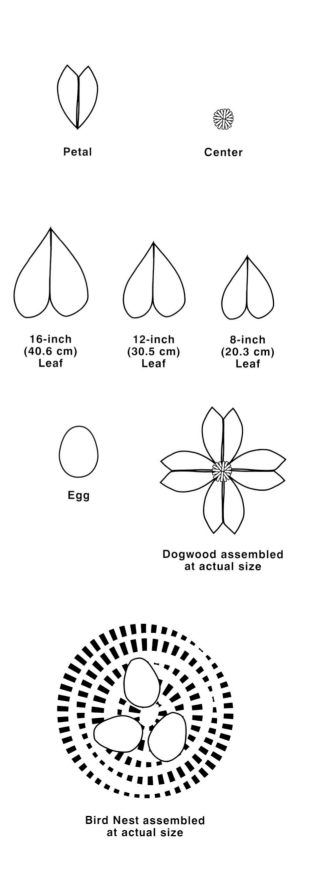

Petal

Center

16-inch
(40.6 cm)
Leaf

12-inch
(30.5 cm)
Leaf

8-inch
(20.3 cm)
Leaf

Egg

Dogwood assembled
at actual size

Bird Nest assembled
at actual size

Water Lily

The sight of a pond filled with water lilies is always awe-inspiring. If you make your own water lily, you may attract a frog . . . and we all know what frogs can turn into.

53

WHAT YOU NEED

- Templates (page 55)
- Basic Quilling Toolbox (page 10)
- ⅛-inch (3 mm) quilling paper: white, pink, light pink, and forest green
- ¼-inch (6 mm) quilling paper: yellow
- Dome-shaped mold (or shallow round container)

QUILLING SHAPES   Marquise    Triangle

WHAT YOU DO

1. To make uniform-size petals, use a circle template board. Roll loose circles for each of the following layers:
   Layer 1 – Roll ten 16-inch (40.6 cm) lengths of the white quilling strips into loose circles, ¾-inch (2 cm) in diameter.
   Layer 2 – Roll eight 12-inch (30.5 cm) lengths of the light pink quilling strips into loose circles, ⅝-inch (1.6 cm) in diameter.
   Layer 3 – Roll six 8-inch (20.3 cm) lengths of pink strips into loose circles, ½-inch (1.3 cm) in diameter.

2. Pinch each loose circle into a marquise.

3. Glue the white layer of marquises together so they lie flat.

4. Glue the two pink layers of marquises together using the cupping technique (page 14).

5. Using the photo for reference, stack and glue the petal layers together.

6. For the center, use a ¼-inch- (6 mm) wide strip of the yellow quilling paper and fringe a 2-inch (5 cm) length (page 13). Cut one end at an angle. Starting from the short fringed end, roll it into a tight circle and curl the fringes outward. Glue this center to the flower.

7. For the lily pad, use a 16-inch (40.6 cm) length of the forest green quilling paper to make a 12-looped wheatear (page 16) using a comb or pattern. Make eight wheatears, and pinch them into triangles. Roll a 4-inch (10 cm) length of forest green into a loose circle for the center. Glue the triangles around the center. Wrap a strip of forest green around the loops and back to the center circle.

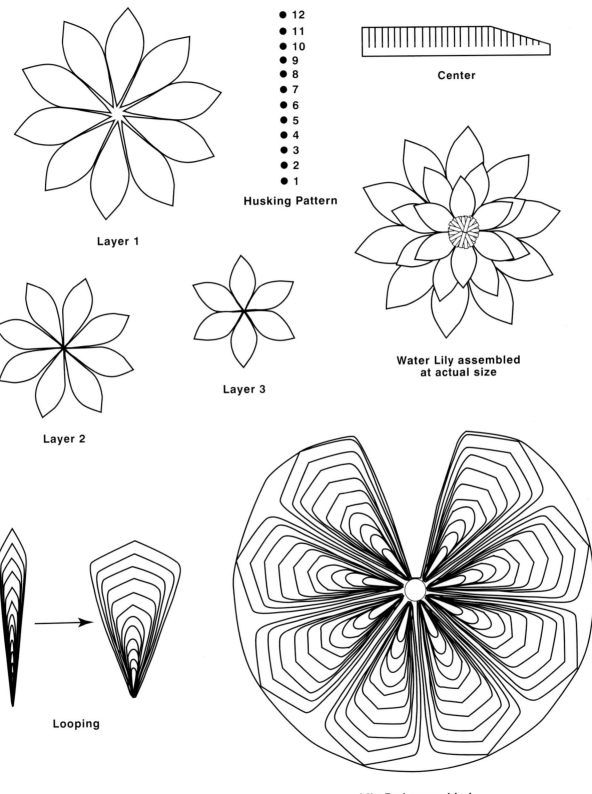

Layer 1

● 12
● 11
● 10
● 9
● 8
● 7
● 6
● 5
● 4
● 3
● 2
● 1

Husking Pattern

Center

Layer 2

Layer 3

**Water Lily assembled
at actual size**

Looping

**Lily Pad assembled
at actual size**

Miniature Rose PLACE SETTING

Perfect for a wedding or a dinner celebration, these colorful roses will add a touch of detail to an elegant table setting.

WHAT YOU NEED

- Templates (page 58)
- Basic Quilling Toolbox (page 10)

- Text-weight paper: yellow, pale yellow, peach, orange, and green

- ⅛-inch (3 mm) quilling paper: moss green
- Decorative place cards, napkin holders, favor boxes

QUILLING SHAPES   Swooping scroll

WHAT YOU DO

1. Cut a 2-inch (5 cm) spiral from the text-weight paper for each rose. Follow the spiral rose technique (page 17) to cut and make the roses. Smaller spirals will make smaller roses.

2. Cut five leaves from the green text-weight paper. Fold each leaf in half to add texture to the leaf.

3. Roll four 4-inch (10 cm) lengths of the moss green quilling paper into swooping scrolls.

4. Glue the roses, leaves, and scrolls onto the place card, napkin holder, and favor box.

tip
You can buy premade die-cuts of spiral roses and be ready to roll in no time.

Leaf

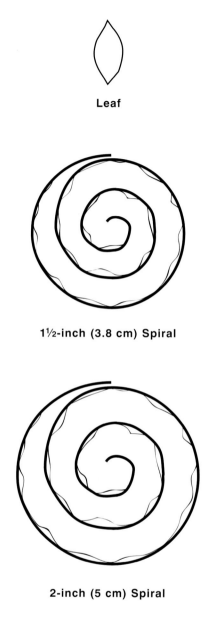

1½-inch (3.8 cm) Spiral

2-inch (5 cm) Spiral

Miniature Rose
assembled at
actual size

Miniature Rose Trio
assembled at
actual size

PRETTY POTTED *Violets*

Roses are red and violets are blue—pretty miniature
potted ones, quilled especially for you!

WHAT YOU NEED

- Templates (page 61)
- Basic Quilling Toolbox (page 10)
- Green modeling clay
- ⅛-inch (3 mm) quilling paper: raspberry, white, forest green, yellow, blue, and purple
- Miniature flowerpots, 2 inches (5 cm) in diameter
- Floral wire (22 gauge)

QUILLING SHAPES   Loose circle   Tight circle   Tight/loose circle

Teardrops   Half Circle   Cone

WHAT YOU DO

1. Place the green clay inside the flowerpots.

2. For one flower, roll five 8-inch (20.3 cm) lengths of the raspberry quilling paper into loose circles, and then form these into five off-center circles (page 13). Wrap a strip of the white quilling paper three times around each off-center circle. Pinch the off-center portion to make an oval petal. Glue three of the petals together. Then glue two more petals behind that assemblage, as shown in the photo and template. Roll an 8-inch (20.3 cm) length of the forest green quilling paper into a cone and insert a wire stem (page 14). Glue this behind the flower. Cut a 2-inch (5 cm) length of the yellow quilling paper in half lengthwise to make two ¹⁄₁₆-inch- (1.5 mm) wide strips (page 15). Cut three 1-inch (2.5 cm) lengths from this narrow strip and then roll each into a tight circle. Glue the tight circles to the center of the flower. Make three flowers for each pot and set aside.

3. For each bud, roll two 8-inch (20.3 cm) lengths of raspberry into tight/loose circles. Pinch them into teardrops and glue them together, using the template for reference. Roll an 8-inch (20.3 cm) length of forest green into a cone and insert a wire stem (page 14). Glue the point of the bud into the cone.

4. For each leaf, roll four 16-inch (20.3 cm) lengths of forest green into half circles. Using Template Ⓐ for reference, glue the half circles together and wrap a forest green strip around the assemblage three times. Make six leaves and spread glue on their backs to support the coils (page 15). Glue them in two offset stacks of three leaves each, as shown in the template. Bend a length of floral wire into a hairpin shape and use it to secure the leaves to the clay.

5. Insert the violets between the leaves' coils and into the clay.

6. Repeat steps 1 through 5 to make the blue violets, but use the blue quilling paper in place of the raspberry and the purple qulling paper in place of the white.

PRETTY POTTED VIOLETS

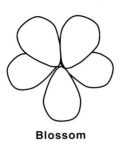

Blossom

Center

Bud

Cone

A Wrapping a Leaf

**Violets assembled
at actual size**

Climbing Roses CARD

There's something so nostalgic and charming about roses climbing a trellis. And the two techniques for creating this card—spiral roses and trellis sticks—are among the easiest to learn.

WHAT YOU NEED

- Templates (page 64)
- Basic Quilling Toolbox (page 10)
- ⅛-inch (3 mm) quilling paper: forest green
- ¼-inch (6 mm) quilling paper: white
- Text-weight paper (or spiral rose die-cuts): pink and dark pink
- Blank green card (or folded green cardstock)

QUILLING SHAPES   Marquise

WHAT YOU DO

1. Cut three 2 x 2-inch (5 x 5 cm) squares from the pink paper and three 2 x 2-inch (5 x 5 cm) squares from the dark pink paper. Cut a spiral for each rose (page 17) or use spiral rose die-cuts. Smaller spirals will make smaller roses. Make six roses.

2. To make each leaf, roll a 4-inch (10 cm) length of the forest green quilling paper into a curved marquise. Make eight leaves.

3. To make the vine, twist a 16-inch (40.6 cm) length of forest green with the spiral technique (page 13).

4. For the trellis, cut ten 16-inch (40.6 cm) lengths of the white quilling paper, and glue them together using the trellis stick technique (page 15). Cut this into six 2-inch (5 cm) sticks. Glue them together using the photo or template for reference.

5. Wrap and glue the vine around the trellis. Glue the trellis to the center of the card.

6. Arrange the roses and leaves, using the photo or template for reference, and glue them to the trellis.

1½-inch (3.8 cm) Spiral

2-inch (5 cm) Spiral

Trellis

Leaf

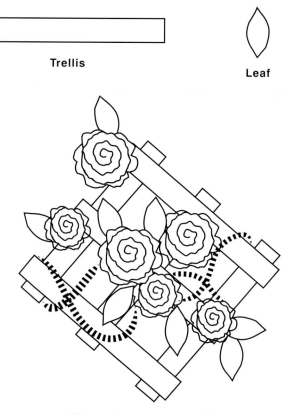

Weave the vine around the
trellis before gluing the
roses and leaves.

Daffodil CARD & GIFT TAG

When you see daffodils blooming, you know winter is almost gone! Use a window cut-out card to frame this flower of cheer and good fortune.

WHAT YOU NEED

- Templates (page 67)
- Basic Quilling Toolbox (page 10)
- $\frac{1}{8}$-inch (3 mm) quilling paper: yellow, deep yellow, and moss green
- $\frac{1}{4}$-inch (6 mm) quilling paper: ivory
- Cardstock: dark green
- Tri-fold card with oval cutout in ivory
- Leaves stamp
- Olive green inkpad

QUILLING SHAPES   Teardrop    Grape roll

WHAT YOU DO

1. To make each daffodil, roll six 12-inch (30.5 cm) lengths of the yellow quilling paper into teardrops. Glue three teardrops together at their wide ends. Glue three more teardrops on top, but spaced further apart, as shown in the photo.

2. To make the center of the flower, glue two 16-inch (40.6 cm) lengths of the deep yellow quilling paper together using the attaching end-to-end technique (page 12). Roll the 32-inch (81.3 cm) length into a grape roll and glue the outside to hold its shape. Fringe a 2-inch (5 cm) length of the ivory quilling paper (page 13), and then roll it into a tight circle. Curl the fringes out and glue it inside the grape roll. Glue the center between the three top petals.

3. To make the stem, curl an 8-inch (20.3 cm) length of the moss green quilling paper into a spiral (page 13). Cut the spiraled strip into a 2½-inch (6.4 cm) length and a 1½-inch (3.8 cm) length.

4. To make the leaves, use a 16-inch (40.6 cm) length of moss green and make a looped wheatear (page 16). Make two leaves.

5. Stamp the card front with the olive green inkpad in a random pattern for embellishment. Rub the ink around the card's edge. Glue the dark green cardstock behind the cutout.

6. Glue the daffodil flowers, leaves, and stems inside the oval cutout.

DAFFODIL CARD & GIFT TAG

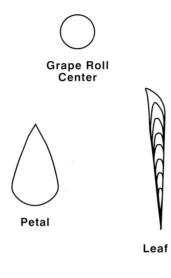

**Grape Roll
Center**

Petal

Leaf

Center

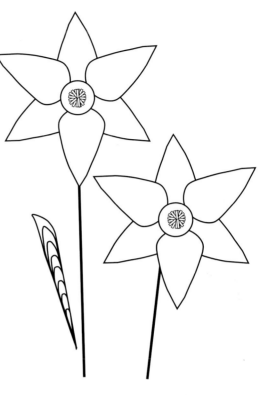

**Daffodils assembled
at actual size**

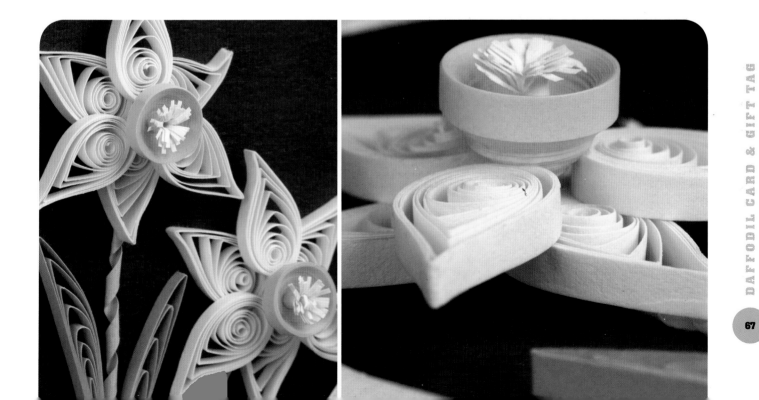

FRAMED Foxglove & Bee

Simple quilled cones become colorful foxgloves even these bumble bees can't resist. Layering strips of slightly different shades of green gives added dimension to the leaves.

- Templates (page 70)
- Basic Quilling Toolbox (page 10)

- ⅛-inch (3 mm) quilling paper: peach, moss green, pale yellow, raspberry, light purple, pale pink, green, black, yellow, and ivory

- Cardstock: dark purple
- 5 x 7-inch (12.5 x 17.5 cm) white frame

QUILLING SHAPES Cone   Marquise Grape roll Teardrop

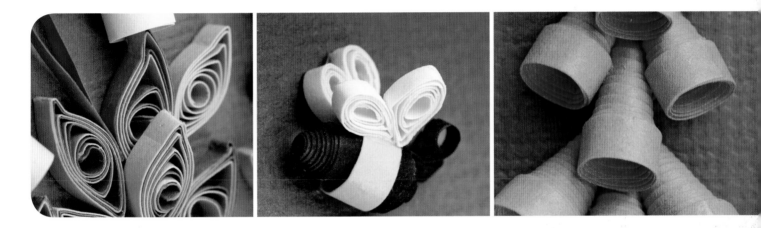

WHAT YOU DO

1. Cut the dark purple cardstock into a 5 x 7-inch (12.7 x 17.8 cm) rectangle that fits inside the frame.

2. To make the peach foxglove, roll the following strips into cones:
   six 8-inch (20.3 cm) lengths of the peach quilling paper
   six 6-inch (15.2 cm) lengths of the peach quilling paper
   three 4-inch (10 cm) lengths of the peach quilling paper
   four 2-inch (5 cm) lengths of the moss green quilling paper

   Glue the pieces together in groups of three, using the template for reference. Starting at the bottom and moving up, layer and glue these clusters to form the flower. Repeat this step to make pale yellow, raspberry, light purple, and pale pink foxgloves.

3. To make the small leaves, roll ten 4-inch (10 cm) lengths of moss green into curved marquises.

4. To make the multi-colored leaves, tear twenty 4-inch (10 cm) lengths of moss green and twenty 4-inch (10 cm) lengths of the green quilling paper. Layer one green strip on top of one moss green strip, and roll into a curved marquise (rolling multiple strips, page 12). Make 10 marquises with moss green on the outer layer and 10 marquises with green on the outer layer.

5. To make the grass, fold a 2-inch (5 cm) length of green in half. Trim the ends to a point. Make eight.

6. Glue the foxgloves, leaves, and grass to the cardstock.

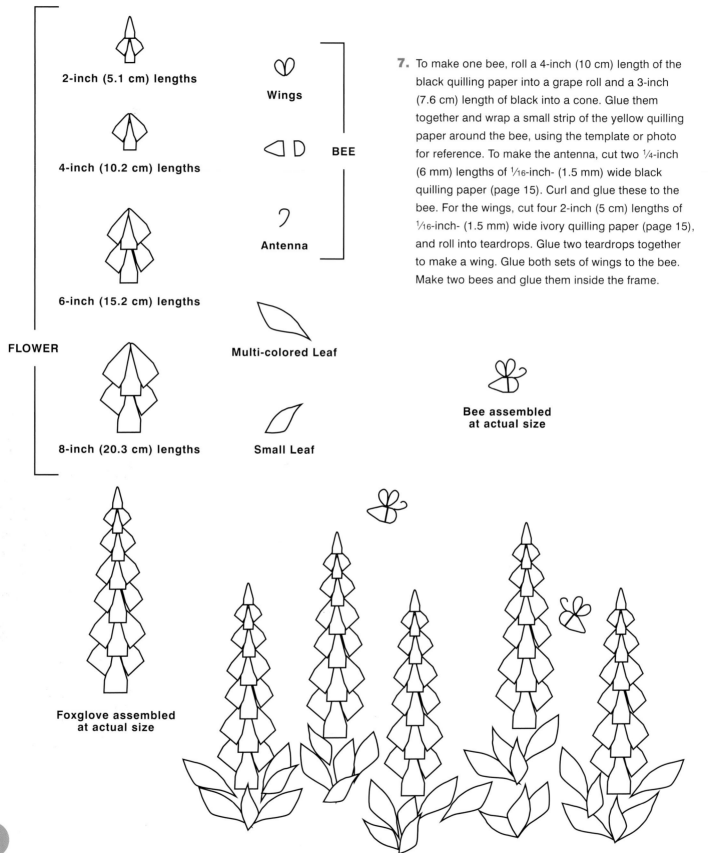

2-inch (5.1 cm) lengths

4-inch (10.2 cm) lengths

6-inch (15.2 cm) lengths

FLOWER

8-inch (20.3 cm) lengths

Wings

BEE

Antenna

Multi-colored Leaf

Small Leaf

7. To make one bee, roll a 4-inch (10 cm) length of the black quilling paper into a grape roll and a 3-inch (7.6 cm) length of black into a cone. Glue them together and wrap a small strip of the yellow quilling paper around the bee, using the template or photo for reference. To make the antenna, cut two ¼-inch (6 mm) lengths of ¹⁄₁₆-inch- (1.5 mm) wide black quilling paper (page 15). Curl and glue these to the bee. For the wings, cut four 2-inch (5 cm) lengths of ¹⁄₁₆-inch- (1.5 mm) wide ivory quilling paper (page 15), and roll into teardrops. Glue two teardrops together to make a wing. Glue both sets of wings to the bee. Make two bees and glue them inside the frame.

**Bee assembled
at actual size**

**Foxglove assembled
at actual size**

Add tall grass in between the foxgloves.

Lilac & Butterfly FRAME

Layered and lightly chalked teardrop shapes cascade gently in this beautiful lilac blossom. For even more elegance, add a gorgeous butterfly with kaleidoscope wings.

- Templates (page 74)
- Basic Quilling Toolbox (page 10)

- ⅛-inch (3 mm) quilling paper: light purple, purple, moss green, blue, light blue, mint green, and black

- Cardstock: dark green
- Purple chalk
- Chalk applicator
- Frame with a 5½-inch- (14 cm) square opening

QUILLING SHAPES Tight/loose circle    Teardrop   Marquise

Off-center circle   Cone

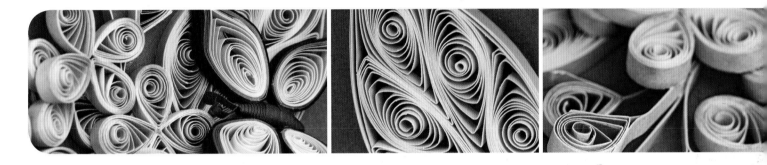

WHAT YOU DO

1. To make each blossom, roll four 8-inch (20.3 cm) lengths of the light purple quilling paper into tight/ loose circles, and pinch them into teardrops. Glue the petals together to make a blossom. Add purple chalk to the petals' tips. Make 14 blossoms.

2. To make each bud, stack and glue an 8-inch (20.3 cm) length of light purple and an 8-inch (20.3 cm) length of the purple quilling paper. Roll the strips with the light purple strip on the outside (page 12). Pinch it into a teardrop. For each stem, fold a 2-inch (5 cm) length of the moss green quilling paper in half. Glue a bud to the stem. Make ten buds and stems.

3. To make each large leaf, roll five 16-inch (40.6 cm) lengths of moss green into marquises. Arrange and glue the marquises as shown in the template and photo, then glue a 16-inch (40.6 cm) length of moss green to one marquise and wrap it around the entire construction three times (see Template). Make two leaves. Repeat this step with three marquises to make the half leaf.

4. Cut a 5½-inch (14 cm) square from the dark green cardstock.

5. Using the photo for reference, arrange the leaves and buds on the cardstock. When you're happy with your arrangement, glue the leaves and buds to the cardstock. Then layer and glue the lilacs to the cardstock. Insert the cardstock into the frame.

6. To make the butterfly's upper wings, glue 8-inch (20.3 cm) lengths of the blue, light blue, and mint green quilling papers together end to end (page 12). Starting from the mint green end, roll it into an off-center circle (page 13), and then pinch it into a marquise. Make two upper wings.

7. For the butterfly's lower wings, glue 4-inch (10 cm) lengths of blue, light blue, and mint green together using the attaching end-to-end technique (page 12). Starting from the mint green end, roll it into an off-center circle (page 13), and pinch it into a marquise. Make two lower wings.

8. Glue one upper wing to one lower wing. Make two sets of wings.

9. For the body, roll two 4-inch (10 cm) lengths of the black quilling paper into cones and glue them together. For the antenna, cut a ½-inch (1.3 cm) length of black and trim it in half lengthwise (page 15). Fold the narrow strip in half, curl the ends, and glue it to the body.

10. Glue the wings and body of the butterfly together. Glue the butterfly onto a leaf.

Blossom

Bud

Antenna

Upper Wing

Lower Wing

Body

A Wrapping a Leaf

Lilac & Butterfly assembled at actual size

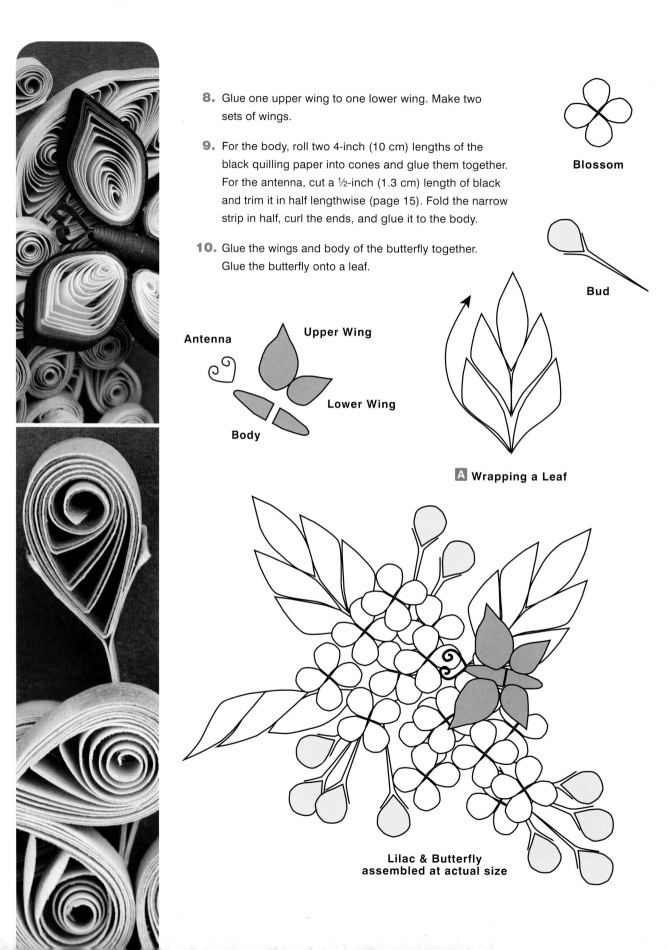

Gerbera Daisy PENS

Use these colorful blooms to play games with
party guests, sign a baby shower book, or just cheer
up your office. They make great teacher gifts too!

WHAT YOU NEED

- Templates (page 77)
- Basic Quilling Toolbox (page 10)
- Text-weight paper: pale yellow (and other colors of choice for petals)
- ¼-inch (6 mm) quilling paper: moss green and deep yellow (and other colors of choice for the centers)
- Ballpoint pen
- Ribbon
- Double-sided adhesive dots
- Thick tacky glue

QUILLING SHAPES Tight circle   Grape roll

WHAT YOU DO

1. To make the pale yellow petals, cut a 1 x 10-inch (2.5 x 25.4 cm) strip of the pale yellow text-weight paper and fringe the entire length using the fringing technique (page 13). Cut the fringe at an angle on one end.

2. To begin making the flower's center, glue a 16-inch (40.6 cm) length of the moss green and an 8-inch (20.3 cm) length of the deep yellow quilling paper together, following the attaching end-to-end technique (page 12).

3. Glue the deep yellow end of this strip to the shorter fringed end of the petal strip. Then, starting from the moss green end, roll the strip into a tight circle. Gently fluff the fringes outward. Shape the tight circle center into a grape roll or a dome that fits around the pen's end.

4. Wrap and attach the ribbon around the ballpoint pen using the double-sided adhesive dots.

5. Attach the gerbera daisy to the pen with the tacky glue.

Gerbera Daisy
assembled at actual size

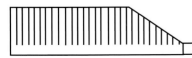

Petals   **Center**

(not to scale)

Peony BOUQUET

78

Peonies are a sure sign of summer and sun-kissed afternoons. Simple V cuts and fringed centers turn a spiral rose pattern into peonies you can bundle nicely into a hand-tied bouquet.

- Templates (page 80)
- Basic Quilling Toolbox (page 10)
- Text-weight paper: shades of pink, orange, yellow, and raspberry
- ⅛-inch (3 mm) quilling paper: moss green
- Yellow chalk
- Chalk applicator
- Floral wire (18 gauge)
- Glue gun and glue sticks
- Green ribbon
- Pins with pearl heads

QUILLING SHAPES Tight circle

WHAT YOU DO

1. To make one peony, cut a 5 x 5-inch (12.7 x 12.7 cm) square from one color of the text-weight paper. Cut a spiral from each square piece, following the spiral rose technique (page 17). Cut small notches in the inner petals on the spiral as shown on the template. Crumple the spiral and reshape. Fringe a 2-inch (5 cm) length at the end of the spiral (page 13). Chalk the fringe on both sides with the yellow chalk. Roll the spiral and glue.

2. For the calyx, roll a 16-inch (40.6 cm) length of the moss green quilling paper into a tight circle. The hole may need to be enlarged for the floral wire. Insert the floral wire with a loop (page 14). Use the glue gun to glue the stem and calyx to the flower.

3. Make a dozen peonies of various colors. Shape the wires into a bouquet and tie with the ribbon. Add the pearl pins to the ribbon as accents.

Cut small notches in the petals as you get closer to the center.

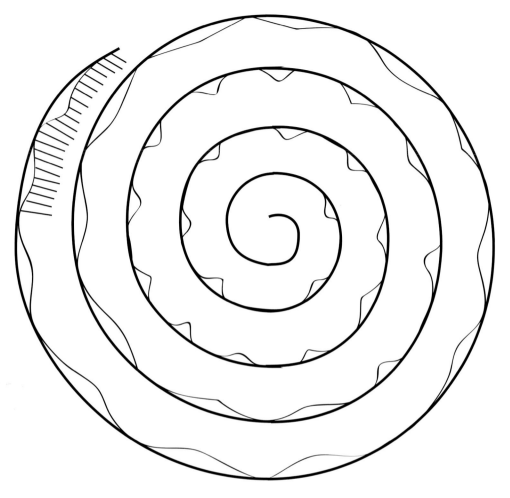

5-inch (12.7 cm) Spiral

**Peony assembled
at actual size**

Ranunculus HAIR COMB

In the language of flowers, a ranunculus says, "I am dazzled by your charms."
Complete your bridal look with this keepsake arrangement of ranunculus
accented with quilled stephanotis you can customize to any color.

WHAT YOU NEED

- Templates (page 83)
- Basic Quilling Toolbox (page 10)
- Text-weight paper: white (pearlized or iridescent)
- ⅛-inch (3 mm) quilling paper: white (pearlized or iridescent)
- Olive green and light purple inkpads
- Hair comb (with fabric covering)
- Jewelry tacky glue
- Pins with pearl heads

QUILLING SHAPES Grape roll (Marquise) Grape Roll (Circle) Double scroll

WHAT YOU DO

1. For the ranunculus, cut a 5-inch (12.7 cm) square from the white text-weight paper. Use scissors to cut a wavy spiral (page 17). Fringe a 3-inch (7.6 cm) length at the outermost end of the spiral (page 13). Crumple and reshape the spiral to soften the paper and to create texture.

2. Rub olive green ink on both sides of the fringed section and let dry. Rub light purple ink on the top edge of the spiral on both sides and let dry. Roll the flower into a spiral rose (page 17). Curl the petals inward. Make three ranunculus flowers.

3. Glue the ranunculus flowers to the hair comb with the fabric or tacky glue.

4. For each stephanotis petal, roll a 16-inch (40.6 cm) length of the white quilling paper into a grape roll and shape it into a marquise. Make five of these petals and glue them together. Roll an 8-inch (20.3 cm) length of white quilling paper into a grape roll and glue it behind the flower. Insert a pin and use the jewelry tacky glue to hold the pin in place. When completely dry, bend the pin 90°. Repeat this step to make another stephanotis. Insert the stephanotis flowers into the hair comb, and glue the stephanotis and ranunculus so their petals touch.

5. Use three 8-inch (20.3 cm) and three 4-inch (10 cm) lengths of white quilling paper. Fold each strip in half and then roll into double scrolls. Glue the scrolls to the ranunculus.

5-inch (12.7 cm) Spiral

Ranunculus assembled at actual size

Stephanotis Petal

Scroll

Stephanotis assembled at actual size

Ranunculus & Stephanotis assembled at actual size

Ranunculus BIB NECKLACE

84

Make a bold yet romantic impression on your wedding day or any special occasion with this floral necklace. The asymmetrical design is very lightweight, and you can easily customize it with other colors and flowers.

WHAT YOU NEED

- Templates (page 86)
- Basic Quilling Toolbox (page 10)
- Text-weight paper: white (pearlized or iridescent)
- ⅛-inch (3 mm) quilling paper: white (pearlized or iridescent) and light purple
- Olive green and light purple inkpads
- Pin with white pearl head
- Jewelry tacky glue
- Necklace chain
- 2 flat, round pendant blanks

QUILLING SHAPES   Grape roll (Marquise)   Grape roll (Circle)   Tight/loose teardrop

WHAT YOU DO

1. For each large ranunculus, cut a 5-inch (12.7 cm) square from the white text-weight paper. Use scissors to cut a wavy spiral (page 17). Fringe a 3-inch (7.6 cm) length at the outermost end of the spiral (page 13). Crumple and reshape the spiral to soften the paper and to create texture. Rub olive green ink on both sides of the fringed section and let dry. Rub light purple ink on the top edge of the spiral on both sides and let dry. Roll the flower into a spiral rose (page 17). Curl the petals inward. Make two large ranunculus flowers.

2. Make the smaller ranunculus with a 3-inch (7.6 cm) square of the white text-weight paper. Use scissors to cut a wavy spiral (page 17). Fringe a 2-inch (5 cm) length at the outermost end of the spiral (page 13). Crumple and reshape the spiral to soften the paper and to create texture. Rub olive green ink on both sides of the fringed section and let dry. Rub light purple ink on the top edge of the spiral on both sides and let dry. Roll the flower into a spiral rose (page 17). Curl the petals inward.

3. Glue the ranunculus flowers to a piece of the white text-weight paper. Trim around the flowers.

4. For each stephanotis petal, roll a 16-inch (40.6 cm) length of the white quilling paper into a grape roll and shape it into a marquise. Make five of these petals and glue them together to form the flower. Roll an 8-inch (20.3 cm) length of white quilling paper into a grape roll and glue it behind the flower. Insert the pin with the pearl head and use tacky glue to hold the pin in place. When the glue is completely dry, bend the pin 90°.

See Ranunculus Hair Comb (page 83) for the 5-inch (12.7 cm) Spiral

5. Carefully insert the stephanotis pin into the outer petals of the ranunculus. Glue the flower petals together to secure the flowers in place.

6. For the lilacs, roll sixteen 8-inch (20.3 cm) lengths of the light purple quilling paper into tight/loose tear-drops. Glue them in groups of four to make four lilac blossoms. Glue the lilacs to the outer petals of the ranunculuses as shown in the photo.

7. Position two pendant blanks far apart behind the floral arrangement. Insert the chain. Check that the chain and pendant's loops (bail) are hidden behind the arrangement, and then secure the pendant blanks with the jewelry tacky glue.

3-inch (7.6 cm) Spiral

Stephanotis Petal

Stephanotis assembled at actual size

Lilac Petal

Lilac assembled at actual size

Smaller Ranunculus assembled at actual size

Ranunculus, Stephanotis & Lilac assembled at actual size

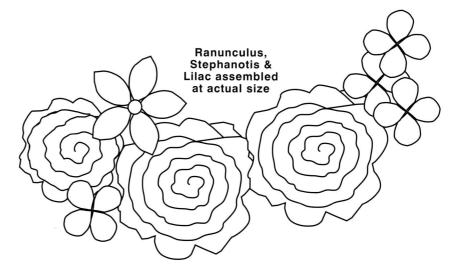

VARIATION FOR RANUNCULUS RING

Transform this lovely blossom into a show-stopping ring: using a double-sided adhesive dot, adhere a single ranunculus flower to the plate of an adjustable 8 mm ring blank.

Lotus

The lotus is a symbol of creation, rebirth, and the sun because it sinks underwater at night, opens again at dawn, and has a sun-like seedcase at its center.

- Templates (page 90)
- Basic Quilling Toolbox (page 10)
- ⅛-inch (3 mm) quilling paper: white, yellow, and forest green
- ¼-inch (6 mm) quilling paper: yellow
- Purple chalk
- Chalk applicator

QUILLING SHAPES   Loose circle   Off-center circle   Marquise

Tight circle   Triangle

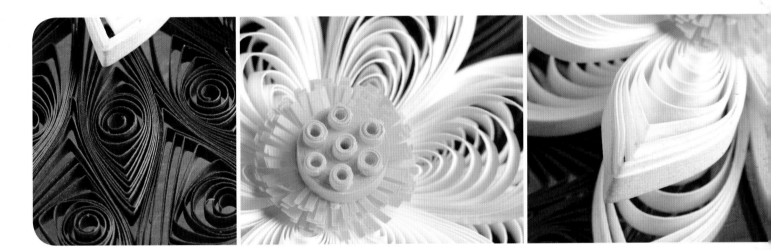

WHAT YOU DO

1. To make uniform-sized petals, use the circle patterns or a circle template board. Roll fourteen 16-inch (40.6 cm) lengths of the white quilling paper into loose circles. Make each into an off-center circle (page 13), and then pinch into a marquise. Glue eight of these petals together for the bottom layer. Glue six petals together using the cupping technique (page 14). Chalk the petal tips with the purple chalk.

2. Using the photo for reference, stack and glue the two layers of petals together.

3. To make the lotus's center, fringe a 4-inch (10 cm) length of the ¼-inch- (6 mm) wide yellow quilling paper (page 13). Measure an 8-inch (20.3 cm) length of the ⅛-inch- (3 mm) wide yellow quilling paper, and glue it to the fringed strip. Roll the assemblage into a tight circle, and curl the fringes outward. Glue it to the center of the flower. Roll a 16-inch (40.6 cm) length of the ⅛-inch- (3 mm) wide yellow into a tight circle. Glue it on top of the fringed center. Cut a 4-inch (10 cm) length of the ⅛-inch- (3 mm) wide yellow in half lengthwise to make two ¹⁄₁₆-inch- (1.5 mm) wide strips (page 15). Cut these into seven 1-inch (2.5 cm) lengths and roll them into tight circles. Using the photo for reference, glue them on top of the tight circle you glued on top of the fringed center.

4. To make the lily pad, roll twelve 16-inch (40.6 cm) lengths of the forest green quilling paper into marquises. Glue them together, leaving an opening between two marquises, as shown in the template. Roll eleven 16-inch (40.6 cm) lengths of forest green into triangles and glue them between the tips of the marquises, using the photo for reference. Roll a 4-inch (10 cm) length of forest green into a loose circle for the center. Wrap a strip of forest green around the loops and back to the center circle.

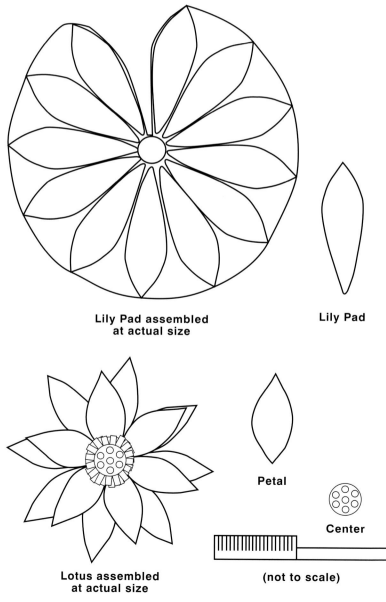

Lily Pad assembled
at actual size

Lily Pad

Lotus assembled
at actual size

Petal

Center

(not to scale)

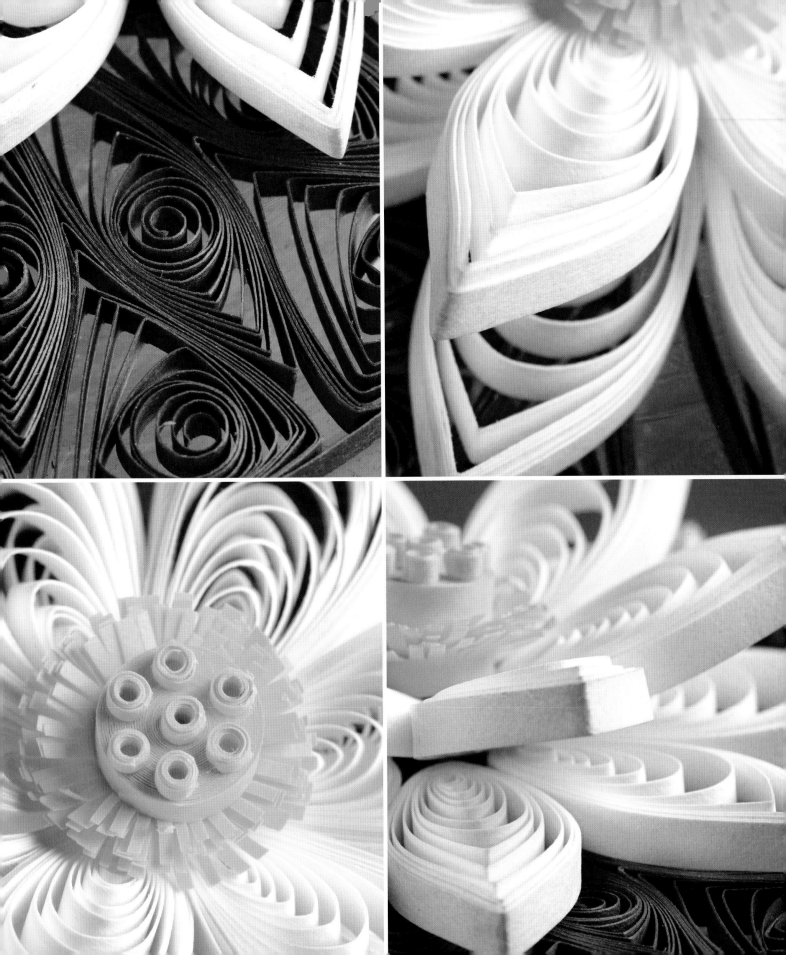

Calla Lily PHOTO ALBUM

Cascading calla lilies make a plain photo album special. Quilling calla lilies is as simple as cutting out teardrop shapes, folding them, and adding tiny quilled cones.

WHAT YOU NEED

- Templates (page 93)
- Basic Quilling Toolbox (page 10)
- ⅛-inch (3 mm) quilling paper: moss green and yellow
- Text-weight paper: white
- Cardstock: dark green
- Photo album with cutout-style cover
- Green and yellow chalk
- Chalk applicator

QUILLING SHAPES Cone

WHAT YOU DO

1. Cut the dark green cardstock into a rectangle that fits behind the album opening. Attach it with glue.

2. To make the calla lily, use the petal template to cut out a teardrop shape from the white text-weight paper. Chalk the rounded end with yellow and green on both sides. Curl and soften the paper with your fingers. Pinch a fold at the rounded end of the teardrop. Place the end of a 3-inch (7.6 cm) length of the moss green quilling paper within the fold, then glue the folded petal closed. Roll a 1-inch (2.5 cm) length of the yellow quilling paper into a cone and glue it inside the lily. Make five lilies.

3. To make the leaves, use 3-inch (7.6 cm) lengths of moss green and trim one end to a point. Make five leaves.

4. Group the lilies and leaves together. Wrap a moss green strip around the stem. Trim the stem bottoms at an angle.

5. Glue the calla lily bouquet to the cardstock.

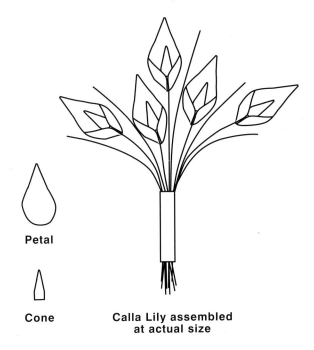

Petal

Cone

Calla Lily assembled at actual size

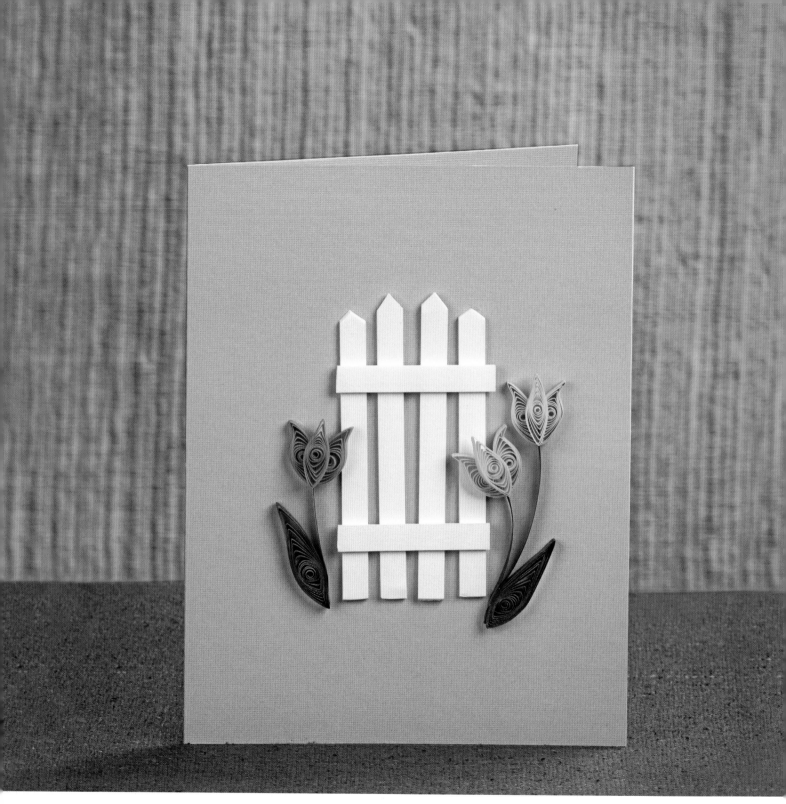

Tulip-at-the-Gate CARD

94

Meet me at the garden gate! Colorful tulips
make this a perfect card for saying thank you,
get well soon, or just thinking of you.

WHAT YOU NEED

- Templates (page 95)
- Basic Quilling Toolbox (page 10)
- ⅛-inch (3 mm) quilling paper: orange, forest green, yellow, and pink
- ¼-inch (6 mm) quilling paper: white
- Folded card: green
- Craft knife

QUILLING SHAPES Marquise

WHAT YOU DO

1. To make the orange tulip, roll three 8-inch (20.3 cm) lengths of the orange quilling paper into marquises. For the stem, glue a 2-inch (5 cm) length of the forest green quilling paper between the two marquises. Curve the points of the marquises out. Using the photo for reference, glue the third marquise on top. Repeat this step to make a yellow and pink tulip.

2. For each leaf, roll a 16-inch (40.6 cm) length of forest green into a marquise. Make two, and glue each to a tulip's stem, using the photo or template for reference.

3. For the trellis, cut ten 16-inch (40.6 cm) lengths of the white quilling paper, and glue them together using the trellis stick technique (page 15). Cut two 1½-inch (3.8 cm) sticks for the horizontal braces. Cut two 2¾-inch (7 cm) and two 3-inch (7.6 cm) sticks for the pickets. Cut the tops of the pickets into sharp points. Glue the fence pieces together.

4. Glue the gate and the tulips to the card.

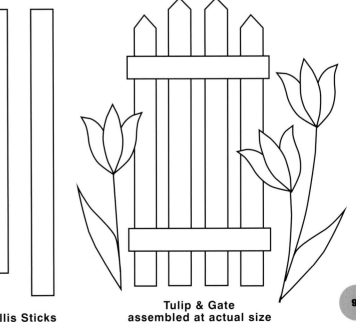

Petal   **Leaf**   **Gate - Trellis Sticks**   **Tulip & Gate** assembled at actual size

95

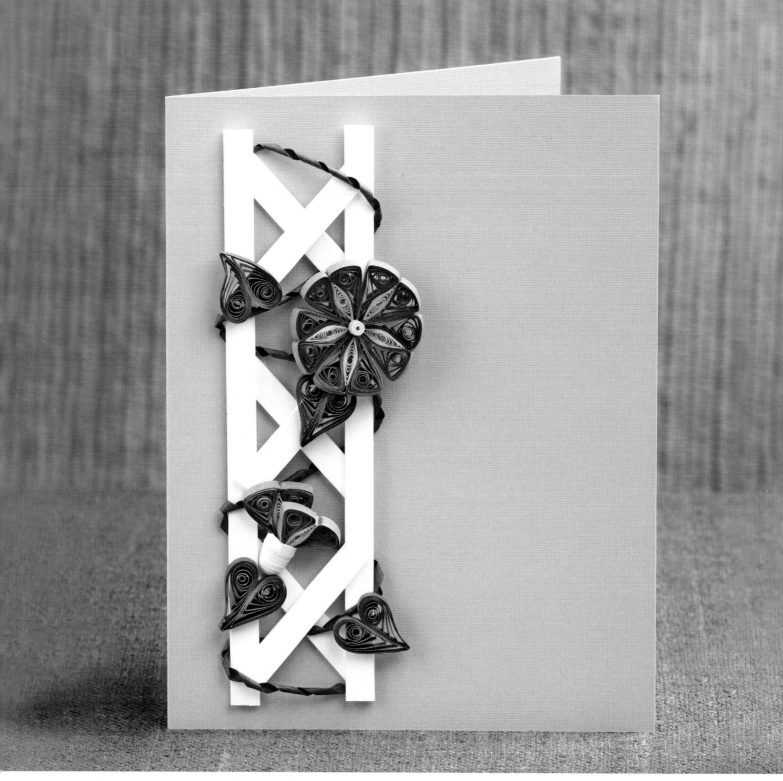

Morning Glory Trellis CARD

The morning glory blooms in the morning, dies by nightfall, but re-blooms the next day. Make a card to let someone you love know you're thinking of them day after day!

WHAT YOU NEED

- Templates (page 98)
- Basic Quilling Toolbox (page 10)
- ⅛-inch (3 mm) quilling paper: blue, light blue, pale yellow, ivory, and forest green
- ¼-inch (6 mm) quilling paper: white
- Green folded card

QUILLING SHAPES   Triangle   Marquise 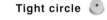   Tight circle ⊙   Cone ◢   Teardrop

WHAT YOU DO

1. For each flower petal, roll two 8-inch (20.3 cm) lengths of the blue quilling paper into triangles. Roll a 4-inch (10 cm) length of the light blue quilling paper into a marquise. Glue the marquise between the triangles to make a petal. Make seven petals.

2. Glue five petals together using the cupping technique (page 14) to form the flower. Roll a 2-inch (5 cm) length of the pale yellow quilling paper into a tight circle and glue it to the center of the flower.

3. Roll an 8-inch (20.3 cm) length of the ivory quilling paper into a cone. Using the photo for reference, glue the two remaining petals into the cone to create the bud.

4. To make each leaf, roll two 8-inch (20.3 cm) lengths of the forest green quilling paper into teardrops. Glue them together and curve a point. Make four leaves.

5. To make the vine, roll a 16-inch (40.6 cm) length of forest green using the spiral technique (page 13).

6. To make the trellis, use ten 16-inch (40.6 cm) lengths of the white quilling paper and glue them together using the trellis stick technique (page 15). Cut these into two 5-inch (12.7 cm) sticks and six 1½-inch (3.8 cm) sticks. Using the photo for reference, place the pieces on the card to create the trellis.

7. Wrap the vine around the trellis and glue it to the card. Glue the trellis to the card, and then glue the flower, bud, and leaves to the trellis.

Petal

Cone

Leaf

**1½-inch
(3.8 cm)
Trellis Stick**

**5-inch
(12.7 cm)
Trellis Stick**

**Weave vine around
trellis before gluing
flowers and leaves on.**

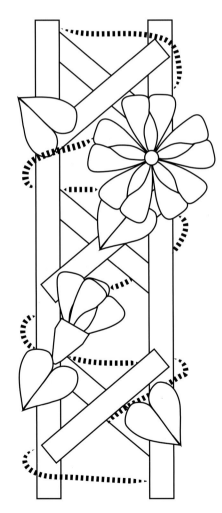

**Morning Glory Trellis
assembled at actual size**

Hibiscus

Bring a little tropical paradise into your home with stunning hibiscus blooms. Marquises and looped wheatears show off the delicate beauty of each petal.

- Templates (page 101)
- Basic Quilling Toolbox (page 10)
- For the orange hibiscus: ⅛-inch (3 mm) quilling paper: pink and orange ¼-inch (6mm) quilling paper: yellow

- For the lavender hibiscus: ⅛-inch (3 mm) quilling paper: raspberry, light purple, and orange ¼-inch (6 mm) quilling paper: yellow and white

- For the red hibiscus: ⅛-inch (3 mm) quilling paper: pale pink, dark red, and red ¼-inch (6 mm) quilling paper: yellow and dark yellow
- Floral wire (18 gauge)
- Glue gun and glue sticks

QUILLING SHAPES   Marquise   Crescent   Cone   Grape roll

WHAT YOU DO

1. For each petal in the orange hibiscus, roll two 8-inch (20.3 cm) lengths of the pink quilling paper into marquises. Glue them together. Then roll six 16-inch (40.6 cm) lengths of the orange quilling paper into crescents. Use the looping technique (page 16) to make a three-part loop with pink paper. Using the template for reference, place the pink loops between the crescents. Glue the assemblage together, and then wrap the entire piece three times with an orange strip (see Template A). Try to wrap tightly with a point at the base of the petal. Make five petals. Use the cupping technique to glue the petals together (page 14).

2. For the stigma, cut a 4-inch (10 cm) length of the yellow quilling paper, and roll it into a cone. Fringe a 2-inch (5 cm) length of yellow (page 13). Cut the fringe on an angle and roll, starting from the longer

fringes. Glue the end. For the stamens, follow the making stamens technique (page 15) to fold, cut, and roll a 2-inch (5 cm) length of orange. Glue the three stigma and stamen pieces together, using the template for reference. Glue the stigma in the center of the flower petals.

3. For the calyx, glue two 16-inch (40.6 cm) lengths of pink together using the attaching end-to-end technique (page 12). Roll it into a grape roll. Make a loop in the floral stem wire and insert it into the calyx (page 14).

4. Use a glue gun to secure the stem to the back of the flower.

5. Repeat these steps to make the lavender and red hibiscuses.

3-Looped Wheatear

Wrapping a Petal
A Glue looped wheatears in different places.

Wrapped Petal

Stamens

Stigma

Hibiscus assembled at actual size

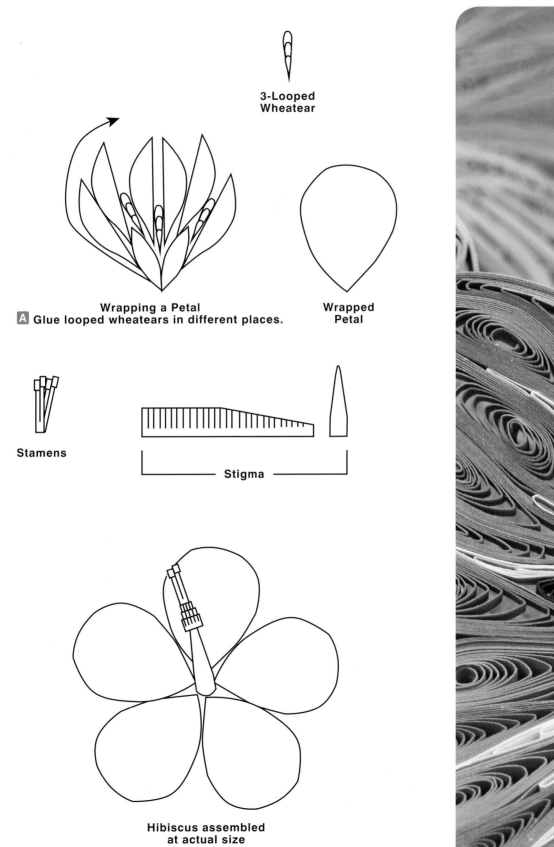

Plumeria Blossoms
CHOKER & EARRINGS

This popular Hawaiian flower is made with gracefully shaped tight circles. Add chalk and accent pearls to create a charming choker with matching earrings.

- Templates (page 104)
- Basic Quilling Toolbox (page 10)
- For the white necklace and earrings: 1/8-inch (3 mm) quilling paper: white and pale yellow

- For the pink necklace and earrings: 1/8-inch (3 mm) quilling paper: pink and ivory
- Floral wire (22 gauge)
- Yellow chalk
- Chalk applicator

- Pins with yellow pearl heads
- Wire cutter
- Jewelry tacky glue
- Jewelry findings (bail, cording or chain, earring backing)

QUILLING SHAPES   Grape roll   Cone   Tight circle

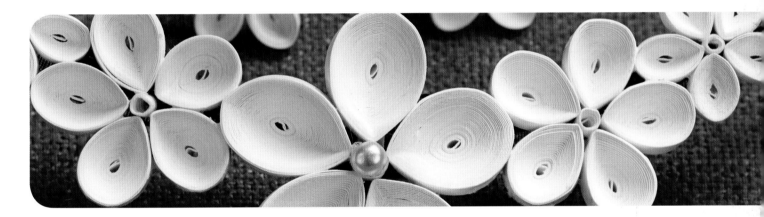

WHAT YOU DO

1. To make the large flower, glue two 16-inch (40.6 cm) lengths of the white quilling paper together using the attaching end-to-end technique (page 12). Roll the 32-inch (81.3 cm) length of paper into a grape roll and pinch it into a teardrop. Make five of these petals, and glue them together to form the flower. Chalk the inside of the petals with yellow chalk. Roll a 4-inch (10 cm) length of the pale yellow quilling paper into a cone and glue it to the center back of the flower. Trim one of the decorative pins with the wire cutters, stick it through the center of the flower, and secure it to the cone with tacky glue.

2. To make each medium flower, roll a 16-inch (40.6 cm) length of white into a grape roll and pinch it into a teardrop. Make five of these petals, and then glue them together to form the flower. Add yellow chalk to the inside of the petals. Roll a 2-inch (5 cm) length of light yellow into a cone and glue it to the center of the flower's back. Make two medium flowers.

3. To make each small flower, roll an 8-inch (20.3 cm) length of white into a grape roll and pinch it into a teardrop. Make five of these petals, and glue them together to form the flower. Chalk the inside of the petals with yellow chalk. Roll a 1-inch (2.5 cm) length of light yellow into a cone and glue it to the center of the flower's back. Make two small flowers.

4. Glue the five flowers together, in the order shown in the photo.

5. Use the jewelry tacky glue to attach three bails behind the necklace. Insert the cording or chain. (Note: You can make your own bail by rolling tight circles with a large hole. Spread the jewelry tacky glue on the paper's edges to stiffen the loop and attach with glue.)

6. For the earrings, make two more small flowers (see step 3). Attach the flowers to the earring backings with jewelry tacky glue.

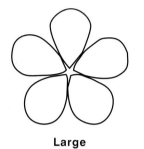

Large

Medium

Cone

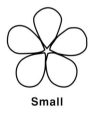

Small

Cone

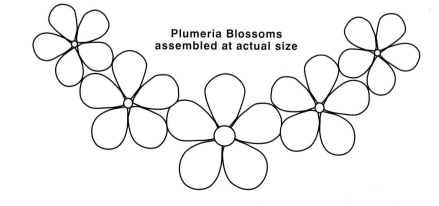

**Plumeria Blossoms
assembled at actual size**

VARIATION FOR THE PINK PLUMERIA NECKLACE AND EARRINGS:

To make a variation of the plumeria necklace in pink, create the large center flower with pink paper and add yellow chalk to the inside of the petals. Make two medium flowers with ivory paper and add pink chalk to the outside of the petals. Glue the three blossoms together as shown in the photo, and follow the instructions in step 5 (page 104) to attach three bails behind the necklace. Insert cording or a chain through the bails.

To make the pink plumeria earrings, follow the instructions in step 6 to create two small flowers with ivory paper. Chalk the edges of the petals with pink chalk and attach the flowers to earring backings with jewelry tacky glue.

Bleeding Heart TREASURE BOX

Filled with romantic letters, cards, and special mementoes, your treasure box deserves to be adorned with a quilled flower that symbolizes undying love.

WHAT YOU NEED

- Templates (page 107)
- Basic Quilling Toolbox (page 10)
- ⅛-inch (3 mm) quilling paper: fuchsia, ivory, and light brown
- Wooden Box

QUILLING SHAPES   **Loose circle**   **Off-center circle**   **Teardrop**   **Marquise**

WHAT YOU DO

1. To make each flower, roll two 12-inch (30.5 cm) lengths of the fuchsia quilling paper into loose circles. Make them into off-center circles (page 13), and pinch a point. Glue them together, using the template for reference. Roll two 4-inch (10 cm) lengths of fuchsia into small teardrops. Roll a 6-inch (15.2 cm) length of the ivory quilling paper into a marquise. Glue the marquise between the small teardrops, as shown in the templates. Glue this to the bottom of the flower. Make three flowers.

2. To make each stem, fold and glue a 2-inch (5 cm) length of the light brown quilling paper to the flower. Make three stems.

3. To make the branch, loop a 16-inch (40.6 cm) length of light brown (page 16) as shown in the template. Bend the top of the loop inward. Make four of these and glue them together to form a branch.

4. Glue the flowers, stems, and branch to the box.

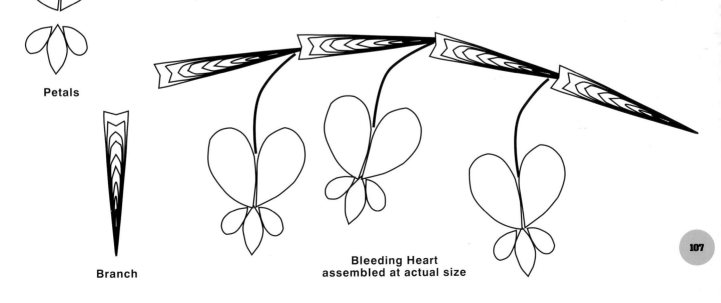

Petals

Branch

Bleeding Heart assembled at actual size

Amaryllis PIN

Add some flare to your holiday attire! Use different shades of red and quilled double scrolls to create a festive, eye-catching pin.

WHAT YOU NEED

- Templates (page 109)
- Basic Quilling Toolbox (page 10)
- ⅛-inch (3 mm) quilling paper: red, dark red, forest green, and ivory
- Pin back

QUILLING SHAPES   **Half circle**   **Marquise**   **Tight circle**   **Double scroll**

WHAT YOU DO

1. To make each petal, roll two 16-inch (40.6 cm) lengths of the red quilling paper into half circles. Roll an 8-inch (20.3 cm) length of the dark red quilling paper into a marquise. Glue them together, using the template for reference. Make six petals, and glue them together in groups of three. Stack the two groups of petals as shown in the template and glue them together.

2. To make the calyx, roll a 16-inch (40.6 cm) length of the forest green quilling paper into a tight circle. Glue in behind the flower.

3. Follow the making stamens technique (page 15) to turn a 4-inch (10 cm) length of the ivory quilling paper into stamens. Glue the completed stamens to the flower.

4. To make one scroll, fold and roll a 4-inch (10 cm) length of forest green into a double scroll. Make four double scrolls and glue them to the flower.

5. Glue a pin back to the calyx.

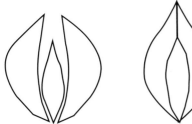

Gluing Pattern

Petal

Stamens

Amaryllis assembled at actual size

Hearts & Flowers
CUPCAKE TOPPERS

Decorate your cupcakes with lovely quilled flowers. They're easy to assemble and make perfect little party favors!

WHAT YOU NEED

- Templates (page 112)
- Basic Quilling Toolbox (page 10)
- ⅛-inch (3 mm) quilling paper: ivory, red, and pink
- Toothpicks

QUILLING SHAPES   Triangle   Teardrop   Loose circle   Marquise   Heart

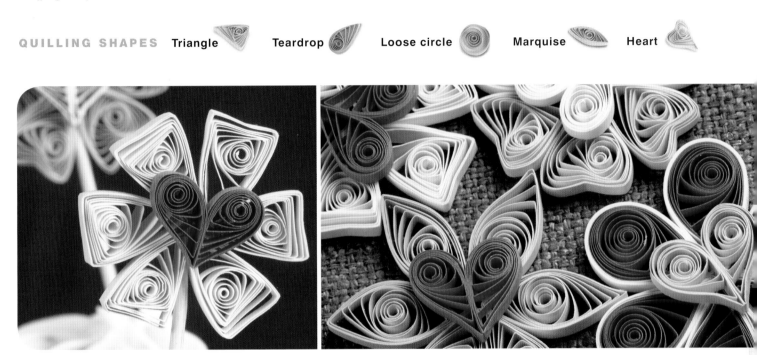

WHAT YOU DO

1. To make the ivory flower, roll six 12-inch (30.5 cm) lengths of the ivory quilling paper into triangles. Glue them together to form a flower, and glue a toothpick between two petals. Roll two 8-inch (20.3 cm) lengths of the red quilling paper into teardrops and glue them together to make a heart. Glue the heart on top of the flower.

2. To make the red flower, roll six 12-inch (30.5 cm) lengths of red into teardrops. Glue and wrap an ivory strip around each teardrop three times. Glue the teardrops together to form a flower, and glue a toothpick between two petals. Roll two 8-inch (20.3 cm) lengths of the pink quilling paper into teardrops and glue them together to make a heart. Glue the heart on top of the flower.

3. To make the two pink flowers, roll twelve 12-inch (30.5 cm) lengths of pink into loose circles. Pinch six of these into marquises and six into hearts. Glue the marquises together to form a flower, and glue a toothpick between two petals. Glue the hearts together to form a flower, and glue a toothpick between two petals. To make the red heart, roll two 8-inch (20.3 cm) lengths of red into teardrops and glue them together. To make the ivory heart, roll two 8-inch (20.3 cm) lengths of ivory into teardrops and glue them together. Glue the hearts on top of the flowers.

Hearts & Flowers assembled at actual size

Anemone

The perfect black-and-white blossom for any black-tie event!
Anemones are a favorite for weddings and engagements
because they complement any flower or cake color.

WHAT YOU NEED

- Templates (page 116)
- Basic Quilling Toolbox (page 10)
- ⅛-inch (3 mm) quilling paper: white and black
- ¼-inch (6 mm) quilling paper: black
- Dome-shaped mold or shallow round container

QUILLING SHAPES   Marquise   Cone   Grape roll

WHAT YOU DO

1. For each large anemone petal, roll six 8-inch (20.3 cm) lengths of the white quilling paper into marquises. Using the template for reference, arrange the marquises into a petal shape and glue them together. Wrap a white strip three times around the petal (see Template **A**). While wrapping, squeeze the marquises flat or re-pinch the points if necessary. Make ten large petals. Glue five of the large petals together using the cupping technique (page 14). Glue the other five large petals together. Spread glue on the back side of the uncupped petals. Using the template for reference, stack and glue the petals with the cupped petals on top. Roll a 2-inch (5 cm) length of white into a cone and glue it to the back of the flower's center. Insert a stem wire through the cone (page 14). Repeat to make two large flowers.

2. For each small anemone petal, roll three 8-inch (20.3 cm) lengths of white into marquises. Using the template for reference, arrange the marquises into a petal shape and glue them together. Wrap a white strip three times around the marquises (see Template **B**). While wrapping, squeeze the marquises flat or re-pinch points if necessary. Make ten small petals. Glue five small petals together using the cupping technique. Glue the other five small petals together. Spread glue on the back side of the uncupped petals. Using the template for reference, stack and glue the petals with the cupped petals on top. Roll a 2-inch (5 cm) length of white into a cone and glue it to the back of the flower's center. Insert a stem wire through the cone (page 14). Repeat to make two small flowers.

(Roses are made with 5-inch [12.7 cm] spiral roses.)

A **Wrapping a Large Petal**

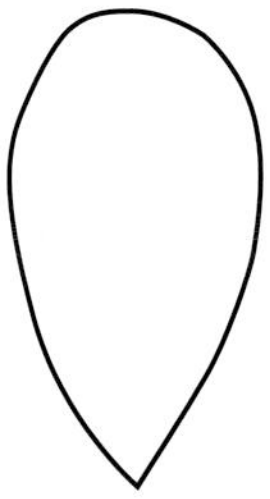

Large Petal

B **Wrapping a Small Petal**

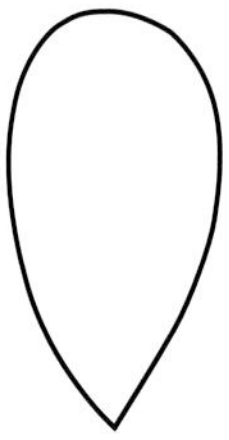

Small Petal

Center (not to scale)

Cone

3. To make the center, fringe a 2-inch (5 cm) length of the ¼-inch- (6 mm) wide black quilling paper (page 13). Cut one 4-inch (10 cm) length and one 16-inch (40.6 cm) length of the ⅛-inch- (3 mm) wide black quilling paper. Cut a 4-inch (10 cm) length of white. Using the attaching end-to-end technique (page 12), glue these pieces together in the following order: 16-inch black, 4-inch white, 4-inch black, and 2-inch fringe. Starting from the 16-inch long black end, roll the assemblage into a grape roll and curl the fringes outward. Glue the center to a flower. Make six centers.

4. Arrange the flowers on the cake.

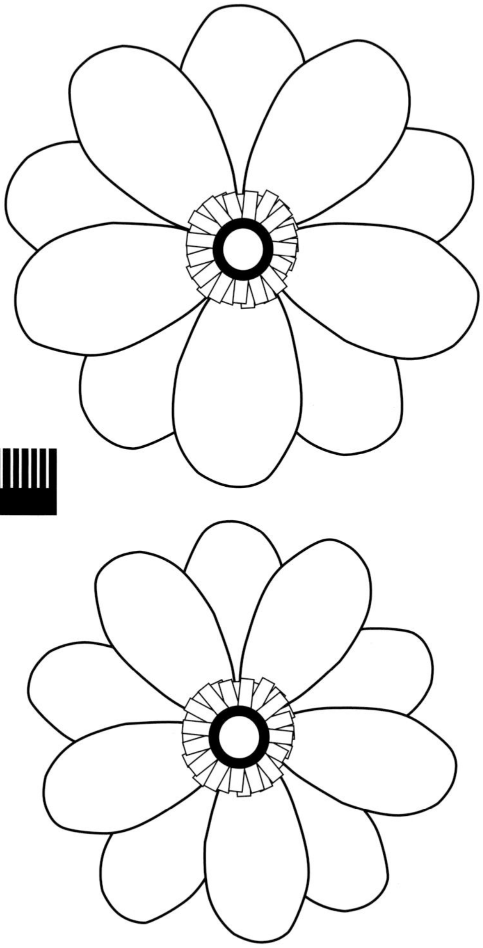

Anenomes assembled at actual size

VARIATION FOR THE ANEMONE

For some added color, accompany the white anemones with pale lavender roses (see page 17), and create a cake-topper arrangement by inserting the floral wires of each blossom into a small dome of polystyrene foam.

Hydrangea PHOTO FRAME

Your favorite photo deserves a special handmade frame. Shade these striking blue hydrangea blossoms with blue chalk to add depth to each petal.

WHAT YOU NEED

- Templates (page 119)
- Basic Quilling Toolbox (page 10)
- ⅛-inch (3 mm) quilling paper: light blue, white, and moss green
- Blue chalk
- Chalk applicator
- 8 x 10-inch (20.3 x 25.4 cm) frame with a mat with a 5 x 7-inch (12.7 x 17.8 cm) opening

QUILLING SHAPES   Marquise    Tight circle ●   Half circle   Double scroll

WHAT YOU DO

1. To make each blossom, roll four 8-inch (20.3 cm) lengths of the pastel blue quilling paper into marquises. Glue four petals together to make a blossom. Add blue chalk to the blossom petals. Make 20 blossoms.

2. For each flower's center, cut a narrow ¹⁄₁₆-inch (1.5 mm) wide, 1-inch (2.5 cm) length of the white quilling paper (page 15). Roll the strip into a tight circle. Glue it to the blossom's center.

3. For each large leaf, roll two 16-inch (40.6 cm) lengths of the moss green quilling paper into half circles, and roll two 16-inch (40.6 cm) lengths of moss green into marquises. Glue them together. Make two large leaves.

4. For each small leaf, roll two 16-inch (40.6 cm) lengths of moss green into half circles. Glue them together. Make four small leaves.

5. For the vines, roll six 4-inch (10 cm) lengths of moss green into double scrolls.

6. Using the photo and template as a guide, glue the leaves onto the mat and then glue the hydrangea blossoms on top of each other in a round shape. Glue the scrolls to the mat.

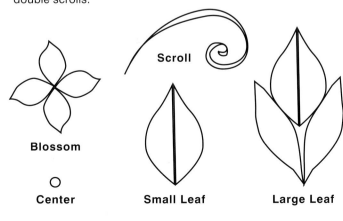

Blossom

○
Center

Scroll

Small Leaf

Large Leaf

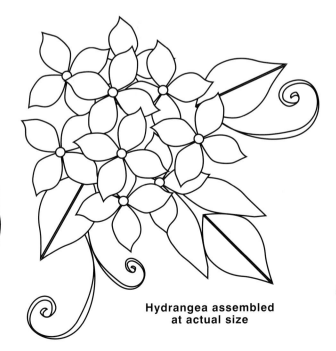

Hydrangea assembled at actual size

Sweet Rose LAMP SHADE

120

Trim a simple lampshade with these dainty roses made of hand-cut paper spirals. In two steps, your ordinary home décor can bloom with loveliness.

WHAT YOU NEED

- Templates (page 121)
- Basic Quilling Toolbox (page 10)
- Text-weight paper (or spiral rose die-cuts): pale yellow
- Lampshade
- Glue gun with glue sticks

WHAT YOU DO

1. For each rose, cut a 2½-inch (6.4 cm) square from the pale yellow paper. Cut a spiral for each rose, and follow the spiral rose technique (page 17) or use spiral rose die-cuts to make enough roses to cover the lower rim of your lampshade.

2. Use the glue gun to attach the roses to the lampshade.

2½-inch (6.4 cm) Spiral

Sweet Rose assembled at actual size

Poinsettia ORNAMENTS

What's Christmas without poinsettias? Make these colorful blooms to bedeck your tree or to add a little handmade cheer to your gifts.

WHAT YOU NEED

- Templates (page 123)
- Basic Quilling Toolbox (page 10)
- ⅛-inch (3 mm) quilling paper: yellow
- ¼-inch (6 mm) quilling paper: red
- Silver thread

QUILLING SHAPES   Marquise   Loose circle

WHAT YOU DO

1. Roll twelve 16-inch (40.6 cm) lengths of the red quilling paper into marquises. Glue six of them together to make a six-petal flower. Curve the points of the petals. Repeat this to make another six-petal flower, and then glue it on top of the first one, using the photo for reference.

2. For the center, roll three 2-inch (5 cm) lengths of the yellow quilling paper into loose circles. Glue them to the center of the flower.

3. Attach the silver thread to one of the petals.

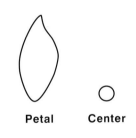

Petal   Center

Poinsettia assembled
at actual size

FRAMED BLACK & WHITE
Chrysanthemums

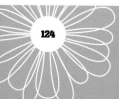

124

A chrysanthemum signifies optimism and joy. The simple layering of solid white pinwheels on a black background is an elegant way to bring good luck to your home.

WHAT YOU NEED

- Templates (page 126)
- Basic Quilling Toolbox (page 10)
- ⅛-inch (3 mm) quilling paper: white
- ¼-inch (6 mm) quilling paper: white
- Black mat
- Frame

QUILLING SHAPES   **Tight circle**   **Marquise**

WHAT YOU DO

1. To make one flower, cut eight 3-inch (7.6 cm) lengths of the ⅛-inch- (3 mm) wide white quilling paper. Glue the strips at their centers to form a pinwheel shape as shown in the templates. Trim the ends to a point with scissors. Curl the points. Repeat this process with eight 2½-inch (6.4 cm) lengths of the ⅛-inch- (3 mm) wide white quilling paper and then with eight 2-inch (5 cm) lengths of the ⅛-inch- (3 mm) wide white quilling paper. Nest the three pinwheels together with the largest on the bottom, and glue them together.

2. For the flower center, cut an 8-inch (20.3 cm) length of the ¼-inch- (6 mm) wide white quilling paper, and fringe the entire length (page 13). Cut an angle on one end. Start rolling from the shorter fringes and roll it into a tight circle. Curl the fringes outward. Glue it to the center of the pinwheel.

3. Repeat steps 1 and 2 to create another flower.

4. To make the side view of the flower, repeat step 1, but fold the pinwheel in half.

5. For the stem, glue ten 16-inch (40.6 cm) lengths of ⅛-inch- (3 mm) wide white quilling paper into trellis sticks (page 15). Cut this into a 3-inch (7.6 cm), a 4-inch (10 cm), and a 5-inch (12.7 cm) piece.

6. For the leaves, roll eight 16-inch (40.6 cm) lengths of ⅛-inch- (3 mm) wide white quilling paper into marquises. Using the photo or template for reference, glue three marquises together to make the small leaf. Glue the remaining five marquises together for the large leaf.

7. Glue the flower, stem, and leaves onto the black mat.

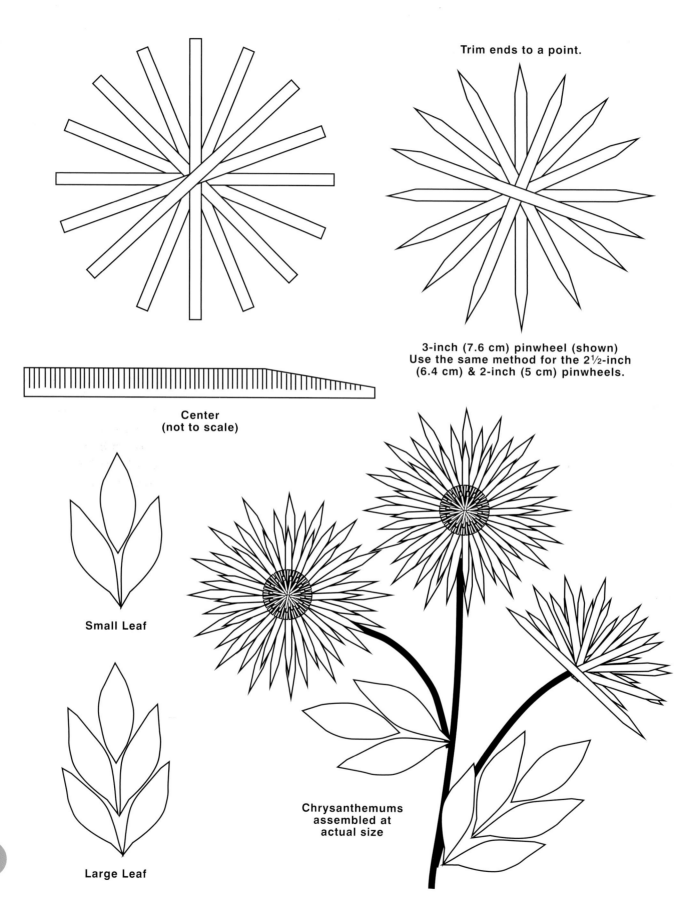

Trim ends to a point.

3-inch (7.6 cm) pinwheel (shown)
Use the same method for the 2½-inch
(6.4 cm) & 2-inch (5 cm) pinwheels.

Center
(not to scale)

Small Leaf

Large Leaf

Chrysanthemums
assembled at
actual size

Acknowledgments

Many thanks to Lark Crafts and Sterling Publishing for having faith that I could create a book on flowers even though I don't have a green thumb!

To my friends and family who shared their favorite flowers with me: Thanks for helping and encouraging me through this process. Knowing "this flower was for you" as I worked on my designs motivated me to quill.

Thanks to my parents, who are amazing gardeners. I could never grow a garden as lovely as yours (but this book comes pretty close). I love you very much!

To my two daughters, Rachel and Kayla, thanks for being so helpful and understanding when Mommy's focus was on flowers. Hope you can see that big projects help us to grow in knowledge and patience. You two are blossoming into incredible crafters and quillers.

Thanks to my puppy, Daisy, who lovingly offered her furry tummy when I needed a break from quilling. I hope you enjoyed eating those scrap pieces that I left for you on the floor!

Big thank you to my husband, Dave, for his loving support. Thanks for keeping our family clean, fed, and functioning while I cut, rolled, and glued during many late nights. I'm so grateful for you! Love you.

Finally, I thank God for creating such beauty in each flower and in each one of us!

About the Author

Allison (Alli) Bartkowski has long been on the forefront of the quilling industry with her creative kits and innovative tools. Her ideas and products inspire others to learn and see beyond simple strips of paper. Her company, Quilled Creations, Inc. (www. quilledcreations.com) is the world's leading provider of paper quilling supplies. Alli is a member of the Craft & Hobby Association and is an accredited member of the North American Quilling Guild. Her projects have been featured in *CardMaker* magazine and can be found on the Quilled Creations, Inc. website. Alli is the author of *Paper Quilling for the First Time*, *50 Nifty Quilled Cards*, and *Paper Quilling Kit for Dummies*. She teaches and shares the art of quilling with crafters around the world.

Index

We Like to Play Music

We Like to Play Music

KATE PARKER

Design by
Zac Parker

HOHM PRESS
Prescott, Arizona

DEDICATION: For Ashe and Zac, the music in my life. And for Lee, the maestro.

Cover design, interior layout and design: Zachary Parker, Kadak Graphics (www.kadakgraphics.com)

All photography taken from stock sources.

Library of Congress Cataloging in Publication Data:

Parker, Kate.
  We like to play music / Kate Parker ; design by Zac Parker.
    p. cm.
  ISBN 978-1-890772-85-7 (trade paper : alk. paper)
  1. Music--Instruction and study--Juvenile. 2. Music appreciation--Juvenile literature. I. Parker, Zac. II. Title.
  MT6.P199 2009
  781.1'7--dc22
                         2008034940

HOHM PRESS
P.O. Box 2501
Prescott, AZ 86302
800-381-2700
www.hohmpress.com

This book was printed in China.

Note to Parents and Teachers

This book was created for the young child (and also for the child within each of us). Small children bring so much joy and curiosity to the experience of sound that it seems only natural to encourage them.

Simply shaking maracas, or orange juice cans filled with beans, to a rhythm can delight children for hours. Dancing around to favorite music can release tension and uplift both children and adults. You don't have to sing like Pavarotti for children to love the sound of your voice. Hearing you sing inspires them to sing along … or alone.

Everyone can play music! Playing music is a way for people to connect and enjoy each other's company. The photographs in this book show a variety of children of different age groups, using different instruments and actually playing music. They show adults and children enjoying music together.

This book can be read or sung to a simple tune that you make up. Talk about the images. Find out how your child or children would like to play with instruments, movement or sound. Then put the book down while you do your own "shaking, rattling and rolling." The text is easy enough to memorize, so let your children read it back to you, again and again. Have a great time.

We like to play.

We like to sing.

We like
to drum.

We like
to ring.

We like to
shake and rattle
and roll.

We like to play music with rhythm and soul!

We like
the beat.

We like
the sound.

We like
music soft.

We like
music loud.

Music connects us and shows how we feel.

Music affects us and can help us to heal.

Music is natural.

Music is grand.

We can make music
by joining a band.

Music is special, however it's done.

You can make
music too,
so join in
the fun!

OTHER FAMILY HEALTH TITLES FROM HOHM PRESS

We Like Our Teeth
**Written & Illustrations
by Marcus Allsop**

Delightful images show baby and adult animals celebrating their own strong, healthy teeth. The clever, rhyming text offers children and parents the basics of good dental hygiene.
ISBN: 978-1-890772-86-4, paper, 32 pages $9.95.
Spanish/English Bi-lingual Version: *Nos Gusta Nuestros Dientes*
ISBN: 978-1-890772-89-5

We Like To Read
**by Elyse April
Illustrations by Angie Thompson**

This vividly-colored picture book provides a new look at how to teach and encourage reading by using play and "attachment parenting" – i.e., lots of physical closeness and learning by example.
ISBN: 978-1-890772-80-2, paper, 32 pages, $9.95. Spanish/English Bi-lingual Version: *Nos Gusta Leer* ISBN: 978-1-890772-81-9

We Like To Move
**by Elyse April
Illustrations by Diane Iverson**

This vividly-colored picture book encourages exercise as a prescription against obesity and diabetes in young children.
ISBN: 978-890772-60-4, paper, 32 pages, $9.95. Spanish Language Version: *Nos Gusta Movernos* ISBN: 978-890772-65-9

We Like To Eat Well
**by Elyse April
Illustrations by Lewis Agrell**

This book celebrates healthy food, and encourages young children and their caregivers to eat well, and with greater awareness.
ISBN: 978-890772-69-7, paper, 32 pages, $9.95. Spanish Language Version: *Nos Gusta Comer Bien* ISBN: 978-1-890772-78-9

TO ORDER: *800-381-2700, or visit our website, www.hohmpress.com *Special discounts for bulk orders.*